FRETBOARD ROADMAPS BEGINNING GUITAR

THE ESSENTIAL GUITAR PATTERNS THAT ALL THE PROS KNOW AND USE

BY FRED SOKOLOW

THE RECORDING
Sound Engineer—Michael Monagan
All Guitar & Vocals—Fred Sokolow
Recorded at Sossity Sound

Editorial assistance by Ronny Schiff

ISBN 978-1-61780-781-7

HAL•LEONARD®
CORPORATION

7777 W. BLUEMOUND RD. P.O. BOX 13819 MILWAUKEE, WI 53213

In Australia Contact:
Hal Leonard Australia Pty. Ltd.
4 Lentara Court
Cheltenham, Victoria, 3192 Australia
Email: ausadmin@halleonard.com.au

Visit Hal Leonard Online at
www.halleonard.com

CONTENTS

INTRODUCTION

The guitar—what a great instrument! You can play any kind of music on guitar: rock, classical, jazz, country, blue-grass, folk, flamenco, pop, and more.

Whatever type of music moved you to buy a guitar, this book will get you started with the basics. You'll immediately learn how to play simple tunes, play basic blues, strum some power chords, play a country guitar lick or two, and even jam with other players. The audio that accompanies this book makes learning easy. Play along with it as you work on each new tune or strum pattern.

Utilizing songs and exercises, and highlighting visual patterns on the fretboard that make playing easier, the *Fretboard Roadmaps* series of guitar books has helped expand the playing abilities of hundreds of thousands of guitarists. This book applies the *Roadmaps* method to absolute beginners, like you, who are looking for your first guitar lesson.

This book and audio will get you started, but once you know the basics, you can move on to one of my intermediate guitar books (approximately one hundred titles are available) or any of the Hal Leonard guitar publications to take your playing as far as you want to go. Whether it's a casual hobby or an obsession, the guitar can be your life-long companion.

Good luck!

THE RECORDING AND THE PRACTICE TRACKS

All of the licks, tunes, scales, and exercises in this book are played on the accompanying recording. It's very helpful to listen to each tune or exercise before attempting to play it.

Some of the tracks are mixed so that the guitar is in one channel (left or right), while the backup band is in the other.

A NOTE FOR BEGINNERS

This book is for beginners—your first guitar lesson. Learning chords, scales, picking patterns, strums, or songs takes a lot of repetition, and every guitarist progresses at his/her own pace. If an exercise or tune seems difficult at first, *don't be discouraged*! Here are some suggestions:

- If a new chord is difficult to play, slowly switch back and forth, in rhythm, between a familiar chord and the new one.

- If a picking pattern or strum is difficult, play it as slowly as necessary, keeping a steady beat.

- If a new technique seems to be far beyond your capabilities, go back and practice the earlier exercises and songs for a few days, then try the new stuff.

- Repeat every new tune, scale, or exercise as many times as necessary to play it cleanly.

- Occasionally, this book will offer both an easy and a more difficult way to play a new chord or strumming pattern. Go with whichever one you can execute. If it's the easier of the two, become comfortable with it for days—or weeks—before attempting the alternative.

- Play every day. Learning guitar is about muscle memory, so you can't "cram" at the end of the week like you might for a test. Even ten minutes a day beats skipping days and making up for it later.

- Use the audio and the book simultaneously and, whenever possible, play along with the recording.

If you follow these suggestions, as well as the tunes and exercises in the book, you'll see real progress. The key is to be patient!

PRELIMINARIES
(BEFORE YOU START PLAYING)

This section covers a few getting-acquainted-with-your-guitar subjects before you start playing.

PARTS OF THE GUITAR

Here are the parts of the acoustic guitar and the electric guitar:

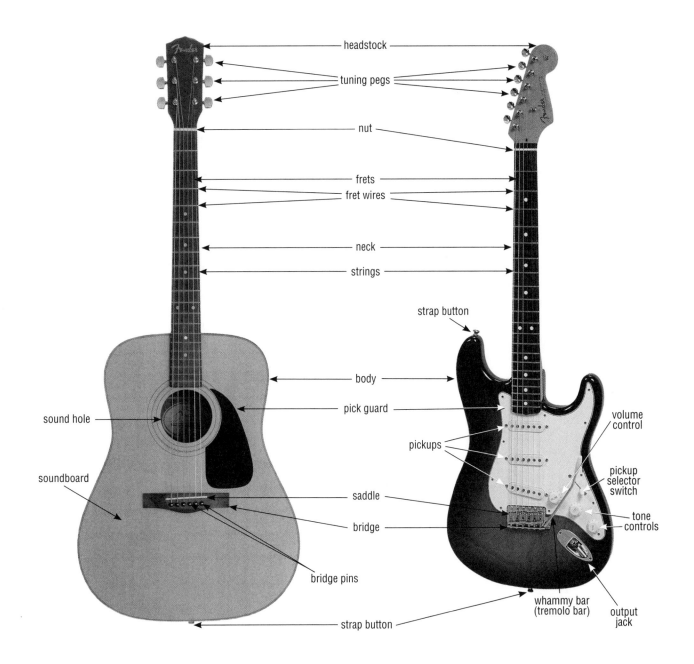

A FEW NOTES:

Bridge: It's attached to the body, and the strings go through it. If there's a separate tailpiece, the strings go through the tailpiece and rest on the bridge.

Fret: A fret is the space between the fret wires, where you'll place your fingers. The first fret is the space between the nut and the first fret wire.

Fret Wire: These metal wires shorten the length of a string when you press down on the fret.

Nut: Typically made out of plastic or bone, the nut is where the strings rest.

Output Jack: A receptacle for a guitar cable, which connects your guitar to an amplifier.

Pickups: A pickup converts the guitar's sound into an electrical impulse so you can plug the guitar into an amplifier. Electric guitars may have one, two, or three pickups. Some acoustic guitars have built-in pickups, which are usually hidden inside the guitar.

Pickup Selector Switch: Electric guitars have many types of switches in various locations on the body of the guitar. Each switch position activates one pickup. Some switches can activate two pickups at once, giving you a combination of two different sounds. When you strum close to the bridge of an acoustic or an electric guitar, you get a harsher, more trebly sound than when you strum farther from the bridge, toward the neck. Consequently, the pickup near the bridge has a brighter sound than the neck pickup.

Saddle: It fits into the bridge and the strings rest on it.

Soundboard: The front of the acoustic guitar's body, which produces most of the instrument's sound.

Strap Button: You can connect a guitar strap to this metal or plastic "button." While most guitars come with strap buttons, they can be easily installed on guitars that come without them.

Volume and Tone Knobs: The amount of knobs on electric guitars is varied, depending on the number of pickups.

Whammy Bar (or **Tremolo Bar**): You can use it to make a note or a chord "wobble" or change pitch. Not all electric guitars are equipped with one, however.

HOW TO TUNE YOUR GUITAR

TRACK 1

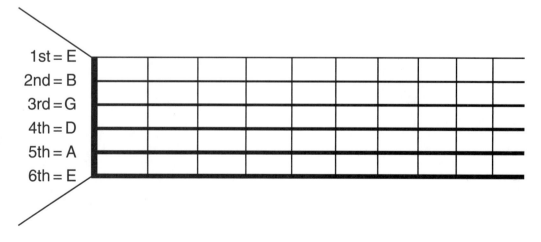

The above diagram illustrates the pitches of each string. Notice that the sixth string is the heaviest (and lowest in pitch), and the first string is the lightest (and highest in pitch).

You can hear the various notes—E, A, D, G, B, and E—on a piano or other instrument, matching each string accordingly. You also can hear the notes on many online sites, such as *tuneyourguitar.com*. Older devices, like pitch pipes and tuning forks, are still useful, but most people favor electronic tuners. Some of these emit tones, while others have dials, gauges, or LEDs that tell you when a string is tuned correctly (you pluck a string and the tuner tells you to raise or lower the pitch). Tuners that clip onto the guitar's headstock are handy, as you don't have to balance them in your lap while tuning.

Turning the guitar's tuning peg one direction *tightens* a string, *raising its pitch*; turning it the other direction *loosens* a string, *lowering its pitch*. Be sure to pick the string before turning the tuning peg, so you can hear how the pitch changes.

The diagram below illustrates the string-to-string method that is useful if you can get a reference pitch for the low E (sixth) string. Then you can tune the fifth string to the sixth string/fifth fret, and so on:

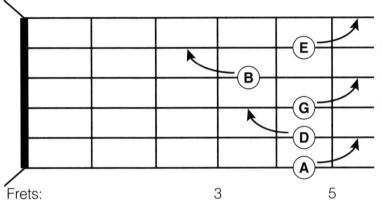

Fret the second string at the fifth fret. Tune the open first string to the resulting E note.

Fret the third string at the fourth fret. Tune the open second string to the resulting B note.

Fret the fourth string at the fifth fret. Tune the open third string to the resulting G note.

Fret the fifth string at the fifth fret. Tune the open fourth string to the resulting D note.

Fret the sixth string at the fifth fret. Tune the open fifth string to the resulting A note.

Frets: 3   5

HAND POSITIONS AND HOLDING THE GUITAR

This photo shows a relaxed way to hold a guitar and a comfortable position for the fretting hand. Your wrist should be straight, not bent in either direction, and the thumb of your fretting hand should rest on the back of the neck.

FRETTING A STRING AND PLAYING CHORDS

The fingernails of your fretting hand should be short, and your fingers should curl over the fretboard so that only your fingertips touch the strings. To *fret* a string, press it down to the fretboard, near the metal fret wire, but not touching the fret wire. If you're not sure where the fret wires are, see the illustration in Parts of the Guitar, page 5.

When you play a chord, such as the E chord in the second photo, be sure that your fretting fingers are arched so that they fret only the intended strings.

Fretting the first string at the first fret

Fretting an E chord

STRAPS AND PICKS

You need a strap to play standing up, and some people find it easier to use a strap even while sitting down (so your fretting hand doesn't have to hold up the guitar neck). Most guitars have strap buttons at two ends of the guitar's body (see the illustration in Parts of the Guitar, page 5) where the strap can be attached. Nylon-string guitars often have only one button—or none at all—but strap buttons can be installed at most music instrument stores.

Picks are not *required*, but they make certain styles of playing easier. They also give you a crisper, brighter, louder sound than your bare fingers.

Flat picks are mostly made of plastic and come in various shapes and sizes. The teardrop pick (see photo—teardrop on right) is the most popular shape, and the photo below shows the best way to hold it. Try strumming down and up repeatedly to get the feel of using a flat pick.

Fingerpicks really save wear and tear on your fingers, if you play a steel-string guitar loudly for any length of time. Most people use metal fingerpicks, which can be bent to fit any finger size, and plastic thumbpicks, which come in different sizes. As shown in the photo, wear the fingerpicks so that they are like "reverse fingernails."

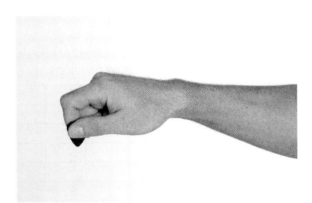 

HOW TO READ CHORD GRIDS

A *chord* is comprised of three or more notes that are played simultaneously.

A *chord grid* is a five-fret representation of the guitar's fretboard. The dots show you where to fret (finger) the strings:

C — Play these strings unfretted (open)

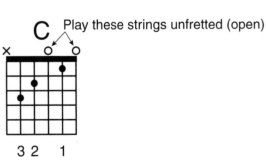

3 2   1

Numbers below the grid indicate the fingering. The number to the right of the grid is the *fret number*.

Dm

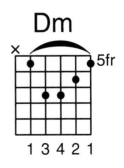 5fr

1 3 4 2 1

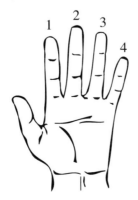

1 2 3 4

HOW TO READ FRETBOARD DIAGRAMS
(THE "ROADMAPS")

Each fretboard diagram is a schematic of the guitar's fretboard as it appears when you look down at it while playing.

- The sixth (heaviest) string is at the bottom; the first (lightest) string is on top.
- Crucial fret numbers—such as 5, 7, 9, and 12—are indicated at the bottom of the grid.
- Similar to chord grids, *dots* on the fretboard indicate where you fret the strings.
- *Numbers* on the fretboard indicate which finger to use (1=index finger, 2=middle finger, etc.).
- *Letters* on the fretboard are names of the notes (A, B♭, C♯, etc.).
- *Roman Numerals* (I, IV, etc.) on the fretboard are *roots* of chords. The root of a chord is the note that gives it its name. For example, a C note is the root of a C chord.

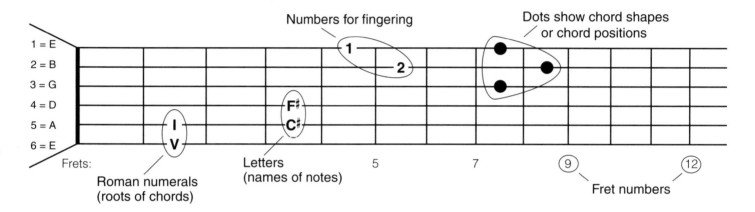

HOW TO READ TABLATURE

Songs, scales, and exercises in this book are written in standard music notation and in *tablature*. The six lines of the tablature staff represent the six guitar strings.

A number on a line indicates which string to play and where to fret it.

Here, the third string is fretted at fret 4:

In this example, the fourth string is played "open," or unfretted:

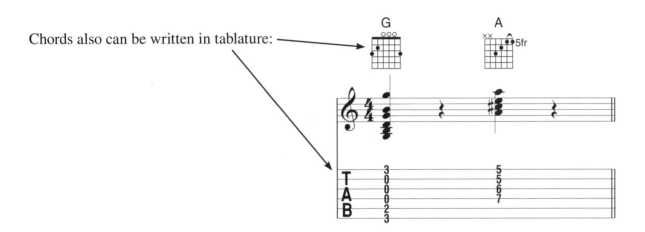

Chords also can be written in tablature:

To get yourself started reading music (standard notation), see the "How to Read Music" section at the back of the book, page 89. Details of tablature notation (hammer-ons, slides, etc.) are explained in the *Guitar Notation Legend* at the end of the book.

WHAT IS A MAJOR SCALE?

(**Note:** If you're anxious to start playing songs, skip ahead to **ROADMAP #3: THE D CHORD FAMILY**. This chapter explains some terminology that is used throughout the book, but you can come back to it later, if you prefer.)

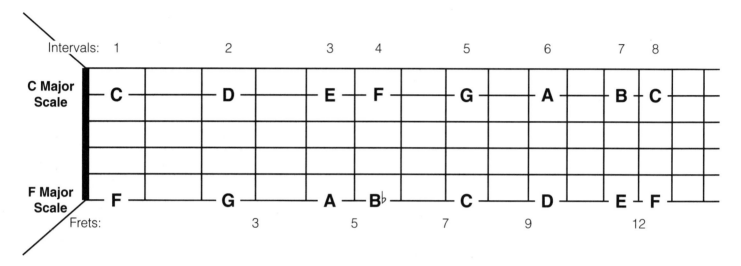

WHY? The melodies to millions of songs are based on it. If you know how to play a major scale, you'll soon be able to play a song "by ear." The major scale is also a ruler that helps you measure distances between notes and chords. Knowing how it is constructed will help you understand and discuss chords and chord relationships.

WHAT? The major scale is the "Do-Re-Mi" scale that you have heard all of your life. Countless familiar tunes are composed of notes from this scale.

Intervals **are distances between notes.** The intervals of the major scale are used to describe these distances. For example, E is the third note of the C major scale, and it is four frets above C (see above). This distance is called a *major 3rd*. Similarly, A is a major 3rd above F, and C♯ is a major 3rd above A. On the guitar, *a major 3rd is always a distance of four frets.*

An octave is the interval of eight notes, including the first and last notes. It encompasses the entire scale. From C to the next highest C is an octave. Notes that are an octave apart sound alike; they are the same note, just at different pitches. In other words, all Cs sound alike, as do all Ds, all Es, etc.

The distance of two frets is called a *whole step*. **The distance of one fret is a** *half step*.

Notes between the letter names are *sharps* **and** *flats*. "Sharp" indicates a fret higher; "flat" indicates a fret lower. The D note is two frets above the C note. The note between C and D can be called C♯ (C-sharp) or D♭ (D-flat).

Chords are defined by their major-scale intervals. A major chord (like C, G, or E) consists of the first, third, and fifth notes of the major scale that is relative to the chord. The C major chord (C) contains a C (I, or first note of the C major scale), E (III, or third note of the C major scale), and G (V, or fifth note of the C major scale). By adding a flatted VII (B♭), the C becomes a C7 chord.

HOW? Play the C major and F major scales that are found in **ROADMAP #2**, starting from the lowest note and ascending, as shown below. Listen to track 2 of the recording, and then play along with it.

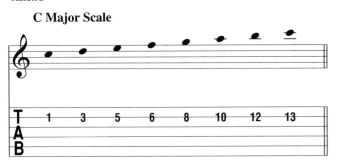

C Major Scale

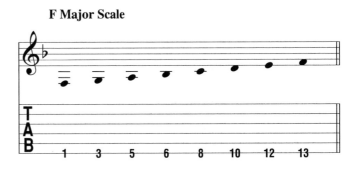

F Major Scale

Every major scale has the same interval pattern of whole and half steps:

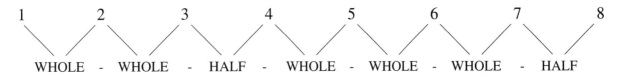

1   2   3   4   5   6   7   8

WHOLE - WHOLE - HALF - WHOLE - WHOLE - WHOLE - HALF

In other words, the major scale ascends by *whole steps* (two frets at a time), with two exceptions: a *half step* (one fret) separates the third and fourth notes and the seventh and eighth notes. This interval pattern makes all major scales sound similar. Playing any interval differently (such as putting two frets between the third and fourth notes) alters the pattern and the sound of the scale. Try it!

Every interval can be described in terms of frets: A major 2nd is two frets, a major 3rd is four frets, an octave is 12 frets, and so on.

DO IT! To learn the major-scale intervals…

Play any note and find the note that is a major 3rd (four frets) higher, a 4th (five frets) higher, and a 5th (seven frets) higher, etc. To do this, count up the right amount of frets on a single string.

Play major scales on a single string. Walk up the string, naming the notes as you go.

SUMMING UP—NOW YOU KNOW…

1. The intervals of the major scale (whole-whole-half, etc.).
2. The intervals that make up a major chord and a seventh chord.
3. How to play a major scale on a single string.
4. The number of frets that separate the notes of each interval (major 3rd, 4th, etc.).
5. The meaning of these musical terms:
   a) Intervals
   b) Sharps/Flats
   c) Octave
   d) Whole/Half Step

THE D CHORD FAMILY

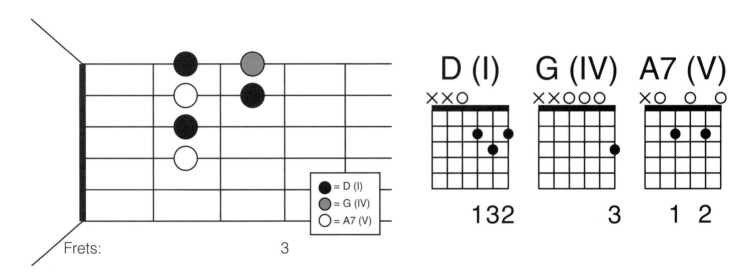

D (I)   G (IV)   A7 (V)

132   3   1 2

Frets: 3

= D (I)
= G (IV)
= A7 (V)

WHY? Every *key* has a "chord family" that consists of three closely related chords—the "usual suspects" for that key. Thousands of songs in the key of D will include the three chords shown above: D, G, and A7. It's practical and helpful to learn chords in families.

WHAT? **Songs are played in *keys*.** A key is like a sonic home base. If a song is played in the key of D major, it almost always ends on a D chord. Playing any chord other than D causes tension, and you resolve the tension by coming back to D, the home base.

Numbers, as well as letters, are often used to describe chords. The numbers relate to major-scale intervals. The first note of the D major scale is D, so, if a song is in the key of D major, D is called the "I chord." The second note of the D major scale is E, so, in the key of D major, an E (or Em or E7) chord is called the "II chord."

The I, IV, and V chords comprise the immediate chord family. In the key of D major, that's D (I), G (IV), and A (V). The V chord is often a seventh chord, such as A7.

I, IV, and V chord changes have recognizable sounds. Eventually, you will know when a song goes from I to V, or from I to IV, just by listening.

HOW? **Play the D chord that is illustrated in ROADMAP #3, above.** Make sure to use the suggested fingering (index finger on fret 2 of the third string, and so on). Strum the top four strings (4, 3, 2, and 1) and make sure each note rings out clearly. Brushing down on a number of strings with a single stroke is called *strumming*. You can strum with your thumb, with the fingernails of your picking hand, or with a pick.

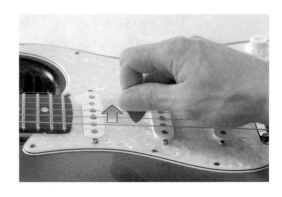

D

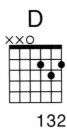

132

Play the A7 chord, using the suggested fingering. Strum all of the strings, except the sixth.

A7

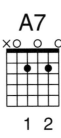

1 2

Practice switching from the D chord to the A7, and back. Notice the similarity between the two chords: to get from D to A7, just *move the index and middle fingers up one string* (from the third and first strings to the fourth and second strings, respectively). These fingerings make it easier to switch from one chord to the other.

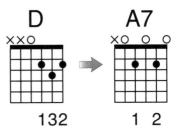

D   A7

132   1 2

To get comfortable with this chord change, strum the D chord three times, then three times on A7, strumming in a steady tempo while switching chords. Don't stop the rhythm of your strum to wait for your fretting hand to catch up. Instead, keep strumming in rhythm, even if the chord isn't yet perfectly formed. Eventually, your fretting hand will learn to catch up with your picking/strumming hand!

Play the G chord. Here, strum just the top four strings (don't strum strings 5 and 6). If the complete, six-string G chord (shown below) is comfortable for you, play it in place of the "starter" G chord.

(starter chord)   (complete)

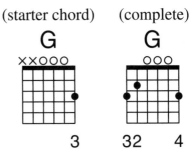

G   G

3   32   4

DO IT! Play the following song, "Down in the Valley." It's a two-chord song, using D and A7. Strum with your thumb, keeping a steady rhythm. Play along with the recording, strumming once for each slash (i.e., three times per measure).

TRACK 4

DOWN IN THE VALLEY
(KEY OF D MAJOR)

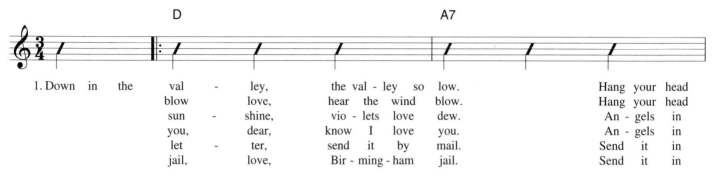

1. Down in the	val - ley,	the val - ley so low.	Hang your head
blow	love,	hear the wind blow.	Hang your head
sun - shine,	vio - lets love dew.	An - gels in
you,	dear,	know I love you.	An - gels in
let - ter,	send it by mail.	Send it in
jail,	love,	Bir - ming - ham jail.	Send it in

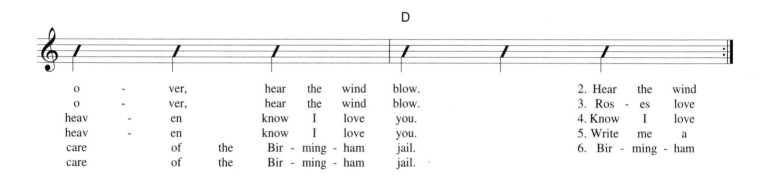

o - ver,	hear the wind blow.	2. Hear the wind
o - ver,	hear the wind blow.	3. Ros - es love
heav - en	know I love you.	4. Know I love
heav - en	know I love you.	5. Write me a
care of the	Bir - ming - ham jail.	6. Bir - ming - ham
care of the	Bir - ming - ham jail.	

Play "Amazing Grace," which uses all three chords (D, G, and A7). Once again, strum down with your thumb (once per measure), keeping a steady rhythm.

TRACK 5

AMAZING GRACE
(KEY OF D MAJOR)

1. A - maz - ing grace,	how sweet the sound that
grace that taught	my eyes to see and
we've been here	ten thou - sand years, bright

saved a wretch	like me.	I
grace my fears	re - lieved.	How
shin - ing as	the sun,	we've

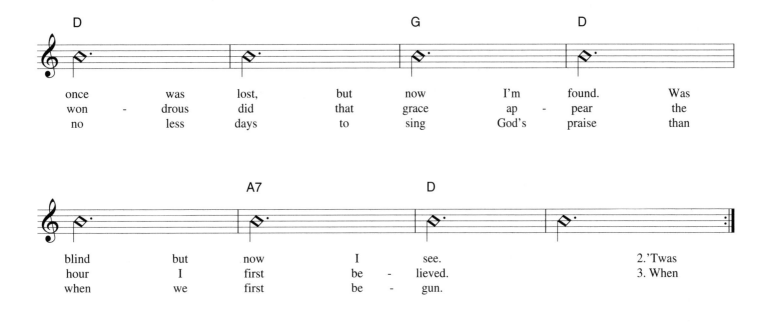

once	was	lost,	but	now	I'm	found.	Was
won - drous	did	that	grace	ap - pear	the
no	less days	to	sing	God's	praise	than

blind but now I see. 2.'Twas
hour I first be - lieved. 3. When
when we first be - gun.

Play "Red River Valley," which is written below. As usual, try to keep up with the recording.

RED RIVER VALLEY
(KEY OF D MAJOR)

TRACK 6
(0:00)

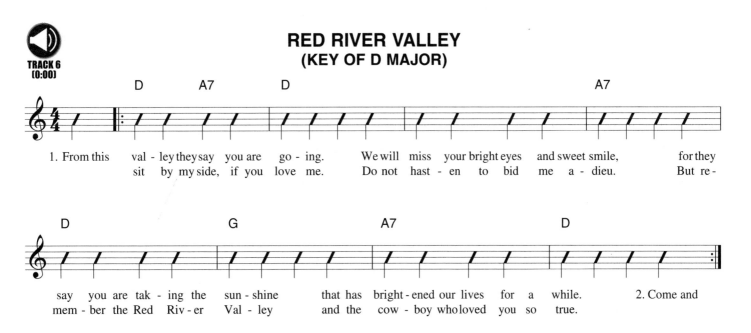

1. From this val - ley they say you are go - ing. We will miss your bright eyes and sweet smile, for they
   sit by my side, if you love me. Do not hast - en to bid me a - dieu. But re-

say you are tak - ing the sun - shine that has bright - ened our lives for a while. 2. Come and
mem - ber the Red Riv - er Val - ley and the cow - boy who loved you so true.

Here's a rock version of "Red River Valley," entitled "Valley Rock." The rock strum consists of up-and-down strokes. For each measure, play eight strokes, or down-up-down-up-down-up-down-up:

$\frac{4}{4}$ 1 ↓ & ↑ 2 ↓ & ↑ 3 ↓ & ↑ 4 ↓ & ↑ ‖

VALLEY ROCK
(KEY OF D MAJOR)

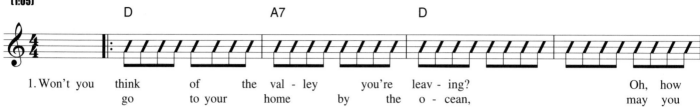

D   A7   D

1. Won't you   think   of   the   val - ley   you're   leav - ing?   Oh,   how
        go   to your   home   by   the   o - cean,   may   you

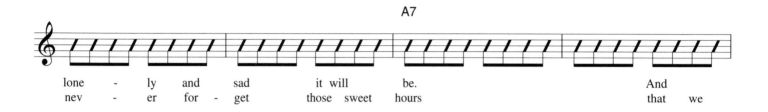

                                       A7

lone - ly   and   sad   it will   be.   And
nev - er   for - get   those sweet   hours   that   we

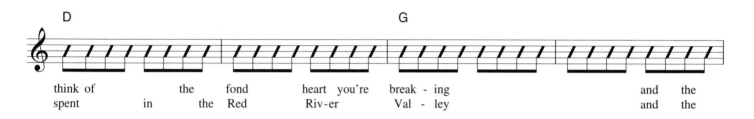

D   G

think of   the   fond   heart you're   break - ing   and   the
spent   in   the   Red   Riv - er   Val - ley   and   the

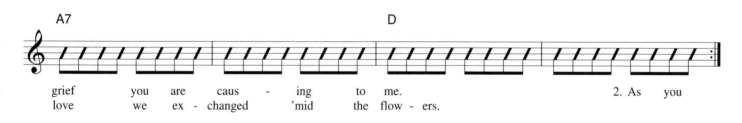

A7   D

grief   you   are   caus - ing   to   me.   2. As   you
love   we   ex - changed   'mid   the   flow - ers.

SUMMING UP—NOW YOU KNOW...

1. How to play D, G, and A7 chords.

2. The meaning of the musical terms "I, IV, and V chords."

3. How to switch from one chord to another and strum a few songs in the key of D major.

4. How to play a basic rock strum.

THE D MAJOR SCALE

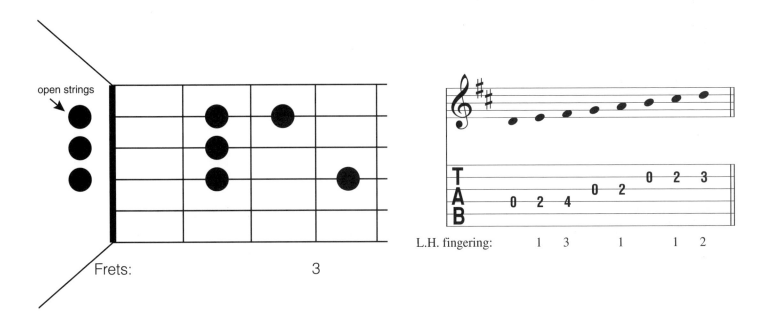

WHY? After you've played the D major scale many times, your hands will know where the notes are located. You'll be able to automatically play melodies by ear, as well.

WHAT? **ROADMAP #4 shows how to play a simple version of the D major scale, using both open and fretted strings.** The black dots comprise the D major scale.

Using the figures below, you can play a second version of the D major scale, which is an octave higher than the first version. It starts with the D note at fret 3 of the second string and continues with the white dots, as shown in the fretboard diagram. Note that this is an incomplete scale, as it ends on the A note at fret 5 of the first string.

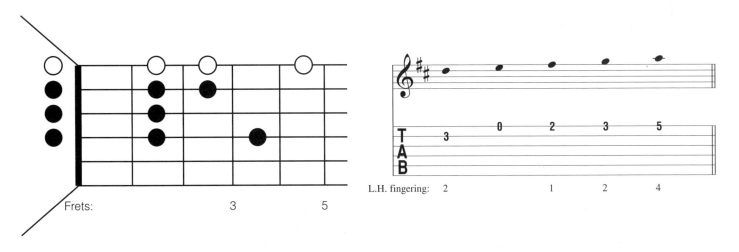

The next example illustrates how to play a lower, descending version of the D major scale. Start with the open fourth (D) string and work your way down the scale, playing the white dots, as indicated in the fretboard diagram. The scale ends on E, one note shy of a complete octave.

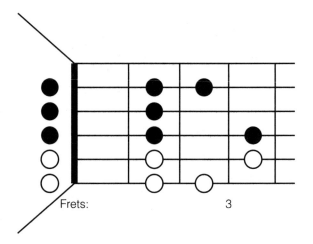

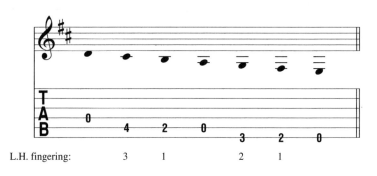

L.H. fingering: 3   1   2   1

 HOW? Play the D major scale, using the left-hand fingering shown in **ROADMAP #4.** Play it up and down, in a loop, as in Track 7 of the recording. As you play the scale, keep your fretting hand hovering over the D chord shape.

TRACK 7
(0:00)

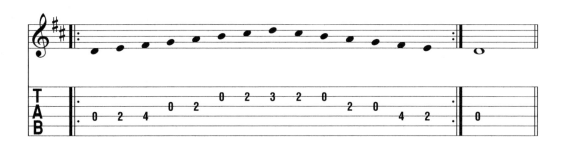

Play this more complete version of the D major scale. Start with the open fourth (D) string and, when you get to the high A note at fret 5 of the first string, go back down, all the way to the open sixth string. Loop it and repeat it over and over, like this:

TRACK 7
(0:30)

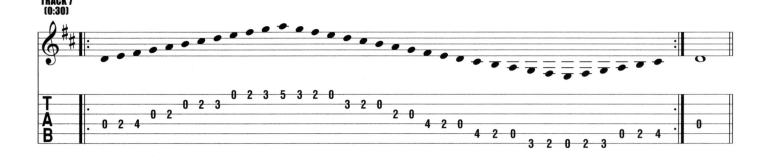

After you've spent several minutes repeating the D major scale, try to pick out some familiar melodies. Go for simple ones that you've heard all of your life, like "Twinkle, Twinkle Little Star" or "This Land Is Your Land." Use the correct fingering: play second-fret notes with your index finger, third fret notes with your middle finger, and so on.

DO IT!

Play the melody to "Down in the Valley." As always, keep your fretting hand in the D chord position and use the proper fingering. Here are two versions, each in a different octave:

DOWN IN THE VALLEY
(MELODY IN D MAJOR)

TRACK 8

Down   in   the   val - ley,   the   val - ley   so   low,

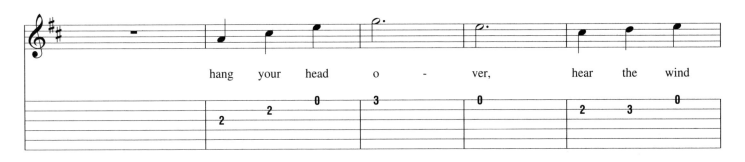

hang   your   head   o - ver,   hear   the   wind

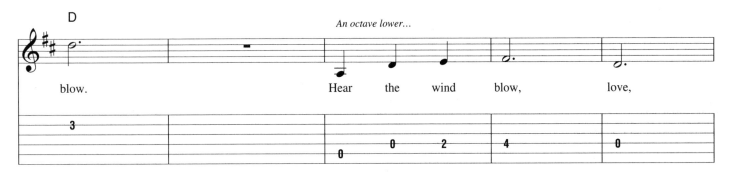

blow.   *An octave lower...*   Hear   the   wind   blow,   love,

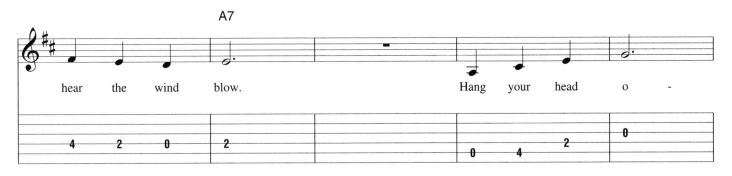

hear   the   wind   blow.   Hang   your   head   o -

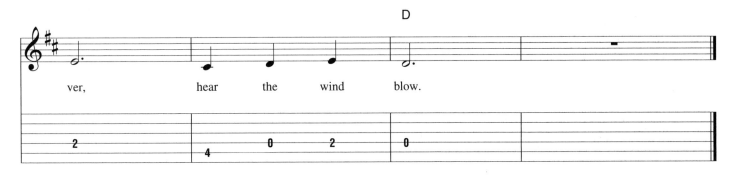

ver,   hear   the   wind   blow.

Play "Amazing Grace":

TRACK 9

AMAZING GRACE
(MELODY IN D MAJOR)

A - maz - ing _____ grace, how sweet the

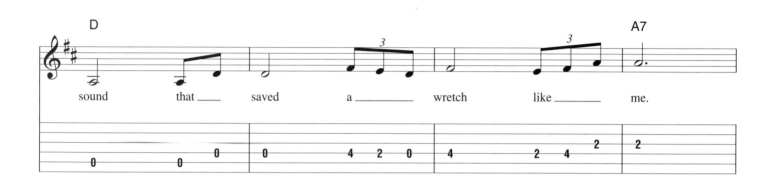

sound that ____ saved a _____ wretch like _____ me.

I ____ once was ____ lost, but ____ now I'm

found. Was ___ blind but _____ now I see.

Here's the melody to "Red River Valley," in the key of D major:

SUMMING UP—NOW YOU KNOW...

1. How to play the D major scale.
2. How to play a few simple melodies in the key of D major.

THE G CHORD FAMILY

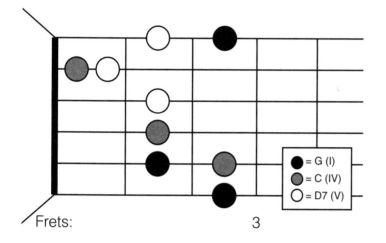

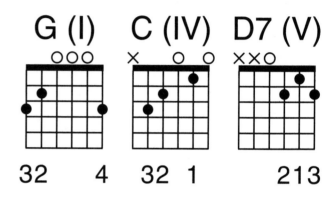

WHY? Once you are familiar with the G chord family, you can play songs in the key of G major, as well as in the key of D major.

WHAT? In the key of G major, G is the I chord, C is the IV chord, and D7 is the V chord.

The chord grids below represent two versions of a C chord: an easy, one-finger C chord and a more difficult, three-finger C chord. If you play the easier C chord, strum the top three strings, omitting strings 4–6. You should try to play both versions of the C chord, however if the "complete" C chord slows you down, play the "starter" C chord in its place.

TRACK 11
(0:00)

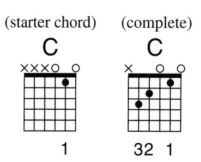

D7 is similar to D major. Although the difference is only one note, you have to completely change the fingering to lower the second-string note:

TRACK 11
(0:09)

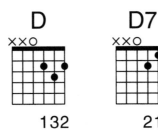

HOW? **Practice switching from one chord to the other.** Strum a G, then a C, and repeat them over and over with a steady rhythm. Do the same with G and D7, and C and D7.

Instead of just strumming chords, try the basic flatpicking strum that is shown below; it's used by folk, country, and bluegrass guitarists:

- Form a G chord and pick the bottom string with your thumb or a flat pick.
- Next, brush down on the high strings (strings 3–1) with your index finger or the pick.

TRACK 12
(0:00)

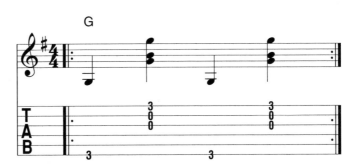

Use the same technique for the D7 and C chords:

TRACK 12
(0:06)

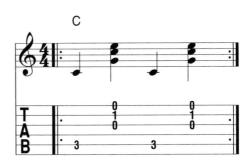

DO IT! Play the following flatpicking-style accompaniment, or "backup," for "Worried Man Blues." This folk-blues was popularized by the Carter Family and has been recorded by countless folk and bluegrass artists. (If the flatpicking strum is too difficult at this point, just strum through each chord with your thumb or flat pick on each beat, like you did in **ROADMAP #3**.)

WORRIED MAN BLUES
(KEY OF G MAJOR)

TRACK 13
(0:00)

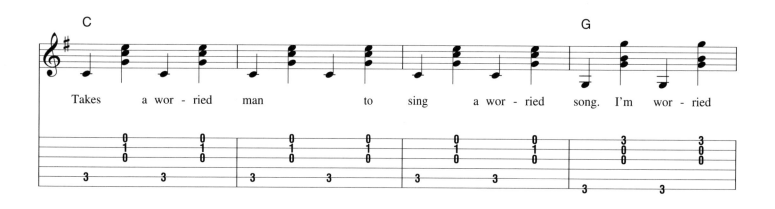

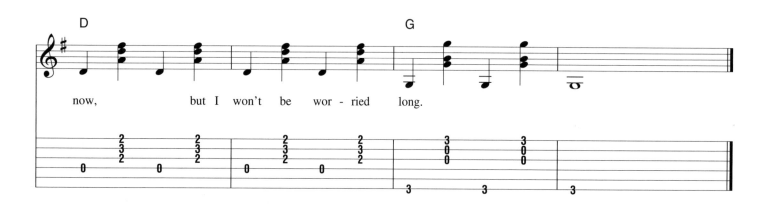

Here's "Worried Man Blues" with a shuffle beat—a rhythmic groove used in rock, blues, and country. Like the rock strum in "Valley Rock" (Track 6), the shuffle beat consists of eight, alternating down-up strokes. As you'll hear on Track 13 (after the flatpicking version of "Worried Man Blues"), the rhythmic feel of a shuffle beat is different than that of the rock strum.

WORRIED MAN BLUES
(BLUES-ROCK SHUFFLE BEAT)

TRACK 13
[0:27]

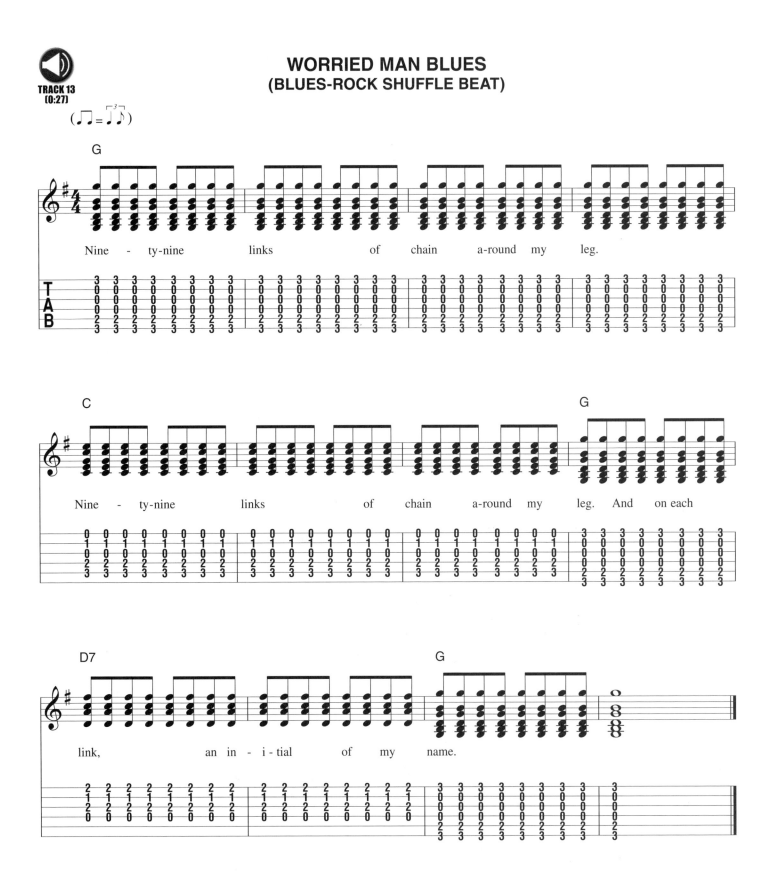

Play "When the Saints Go Marching In," using the flatpicking strum, or just strum through each chord with your thumb or flat pick on each beat.

TRACK 14

WHEN THE SAINTS GO MARCHING IN
(KEY OF G MAJOR)

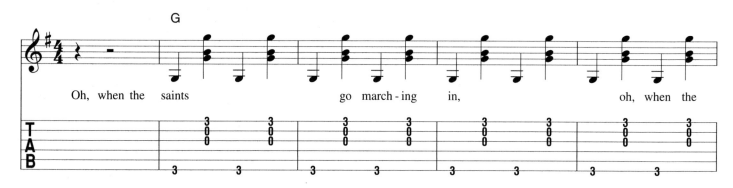

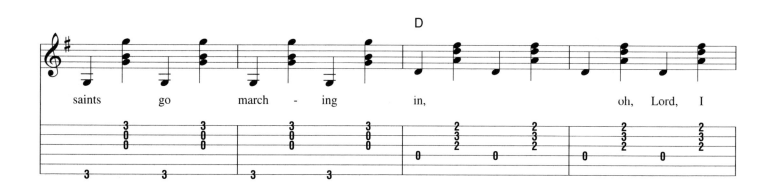

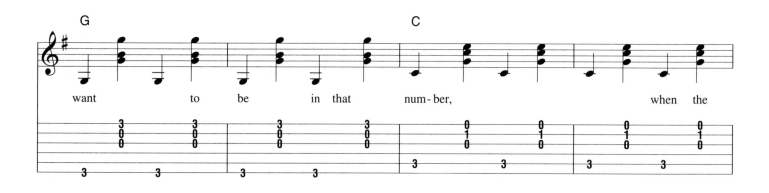

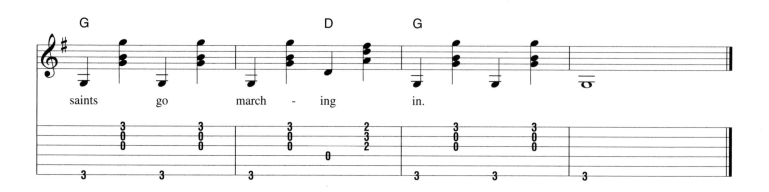

Here's a flatpicking-style backup to "Amazing Grace," in the key of G major. Since the tune is a waltz (in 3/4 time—three beats to a measure), on the first beat, pick a bass note, followed by *two* downward strums, instead of one. Notice the D chord; no rule dictates that the V chord *must* be a seventh chord.

AMAZING GRACE
(KEY OF G MAJOR)

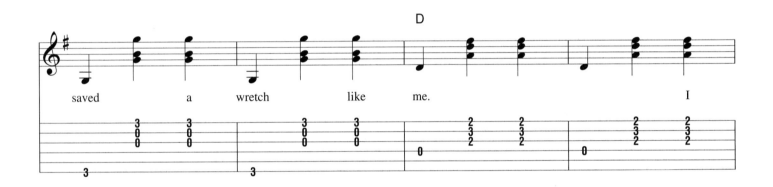

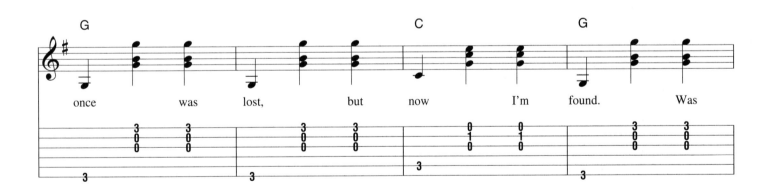

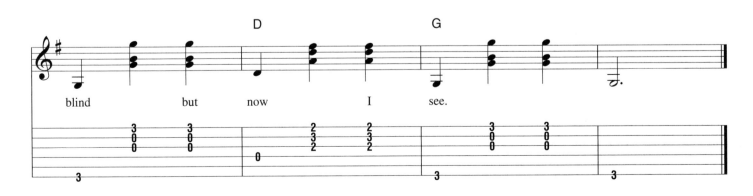

The "straight-eighths" rock feel that is used in the next musical example consists of eight downstrokes per bar. It's a two-chord groove, with the seventh chords giving it a bluesy feel. Strum with a flat pick, eight downstrokes per bar:

TRACK 16
[0:00]

STRAIGHT-EIGHTHS BLUES ROCK

TRACK 16
[0:05]

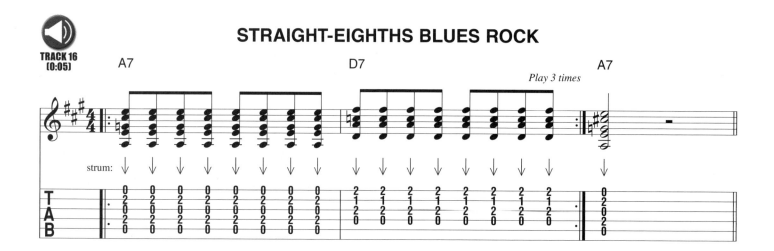

SUMMING UP—NOW YOU KNOW...

1. How to play C and D7 chords.

2. The I, IV, and V chords in the key of G major.

3. The basic flatpicking strum in 4/4 time and waltz (3/4) time.

4. How to switch from one chord to another and strum a few songs in the key of G major.

5. How to play a straight-eighths rock strum.

THE G MAJOR SCALE

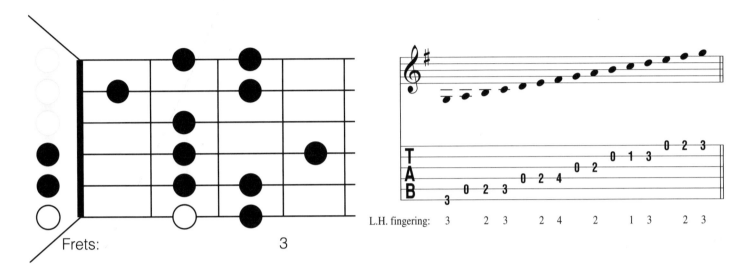

L.H. fingering: 3   2   3   2   4   2   1   3   2   3

WHY? Once you're familiar with this scale, you can play the melodies to countless songs in the key of G major.

V HAT? **ROADMAP #6 is really two G major scales.** Because it includes two complete octaves, you can play songs in two registers—on the bass strings and on the treble strings.

As was the case in ROADMAP #4, the white dots are "extra notes" below the given G major scale. These notes are easy to reach while staying in the G chord position.

The G major scale contains the exact same notes as the D major scale, with one exception: The D major scale includes a C♯ (fret 4 of the fifth string and fret 2 of the second string); the G scale contains a C natural (fret 3 of the fifth string and fret 1 of the second string).

Both scales contain an F♯, however. Of course, the D major scale starts on a D note and the G major scale starts on a G note.

HOW? **Practice the two versions of the G major scale by repeating the following two "loops" several times.**

TRACK 17

DO IT! Once you are familiar with the G major scale, try to play songs "by ear," as you did with the D major scale.

Play the melody to "Worried Man Blues," in the key of G:

TRACK 18

WORRIED MAN BLUES
(MELODY IN G MAJOR)

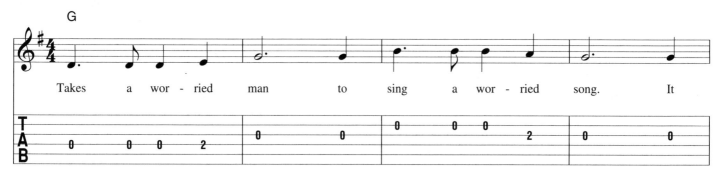

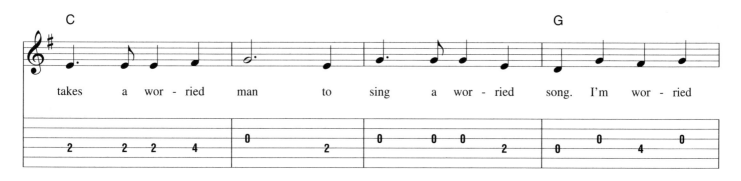

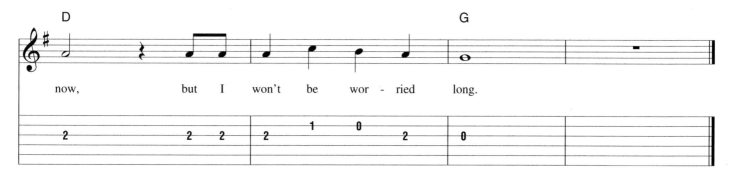

Play the melody to "When the Saints Go Marching In," in the key of G major. The melody jumps up an octave at the song's midpoint.

TRACK 19

WHEN THE SAINTS GO MARCHING IN
(MELODY IN G MAJOR)

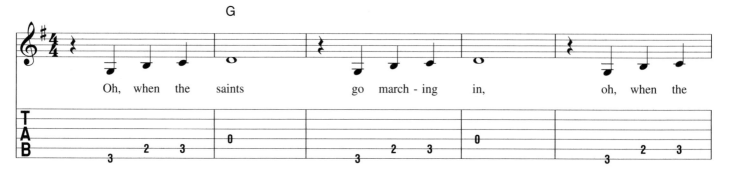

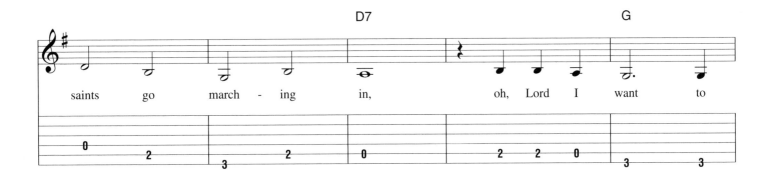

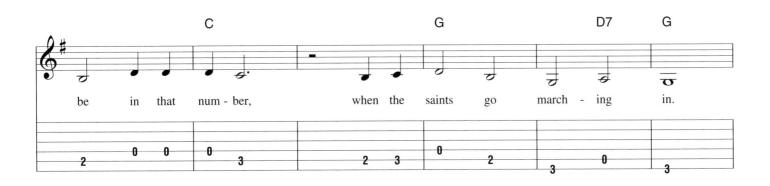

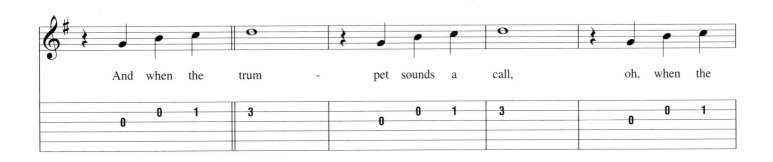

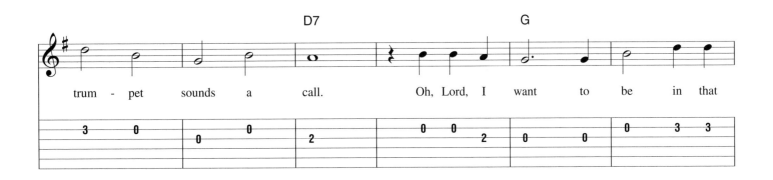

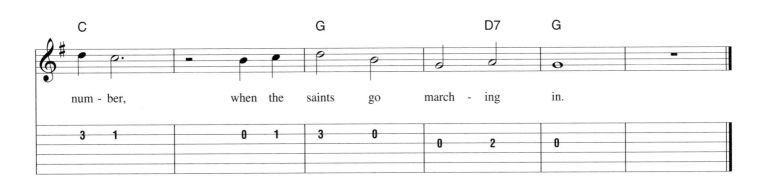

Play the melody to "Wildwood Flower," in the key of G major. This old ballad was popularized by the Carter Family (check out the Johnny Cash biopic *Walk the Line*). Every country guitar picker should know how to play this song!

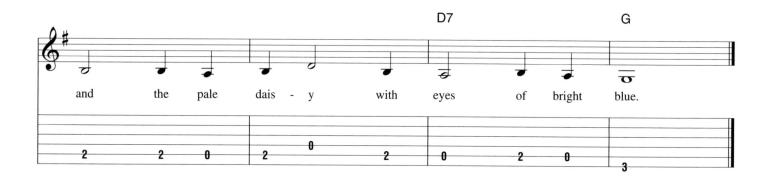

WILDWOOD FLOWER
(MELODY IN G MAJOR)

TRACK 20
(0:00)

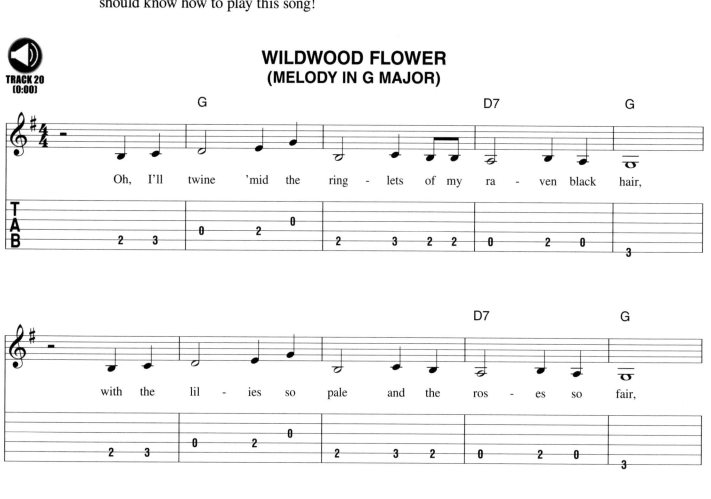

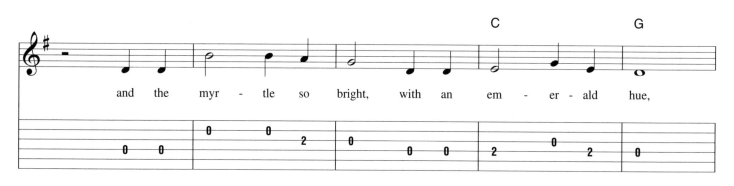

Here's "Wildwood Flower" played "Carter-style." It's the same tune, but when a melody note is sustained (held), you fill in the space by brushing down on the treble strings (strings 3–1) with your flat pick or finger. Make sure you fret the chords as written so the "brush-downs" on the treble strings sound the correct chord.

WILDWOOD FLOWER
(MELODY IN G MAJOR, FLATPICKING STYLE)

SUMMING UP—NOW YOU KNOW...

1. How to play the G major scale.
2. How to play a few familiar melodies in the key of G major.
3. How to play a melody and fill in the spaces with brush strokes on the treble strings, flatpicking-style.

THE A CHORD FAMILY

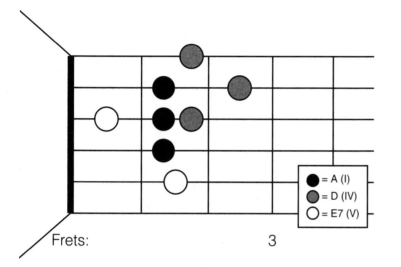

Frets: 3

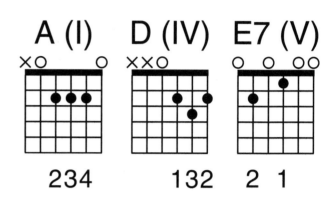

A (I)   D (IV)   E7 (V)

234   132   2 1

WHY? These are the chords that you need to play in the key of A major.

WHAT? **In the key of A major, A is the I chord, D is the IV chord, and E7 is the V chord.**

A is similar to A7, except for the third string:

TRACK 21
(0:00)

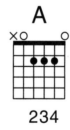 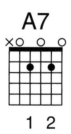

A   A7

234   1 2

HOW? **Practice switching from A to D and back, and do the same with A and E7.** If you use the suggested fingering for A, switch to E7 by moving your middle finger up from fret 2 of the fourth string to fret 2 of the fifth string and add your index finger to fret 1 of the third string.

TRACK 21
(0:08)

DO IT! Play the folk tune "I Never Will Marry," in the key of A major. It's a waltz (3/4 time), so use the same flatpicking backup as found in "Amazing Grace" in **ROADMAP #5** (Track 15).

I NEVER WILL MARRY
(KEY OF A MAJOR, FLATPICKING STYLE)

Play the folk-blues "Careless Love." It has been recorded and performed by blues, rock, country, bluegrass, and jazz singers. This is a flatpicking arrangement, like the ones in **ROADMAP #5** (pick the root bass note, then brush down on the treble strings).

CARELESS LOVE
(KEY OF A MAJOR, FLATPICKING STYLE)

Love,   oh,   love, oh,   care - less   love,

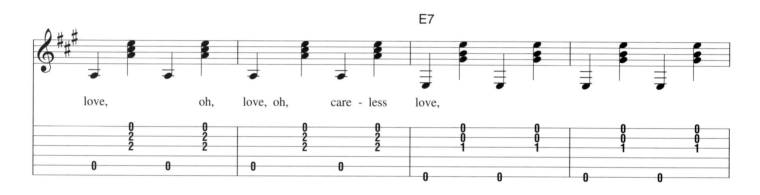

love,   oh,   love, oh,   care - less   love,

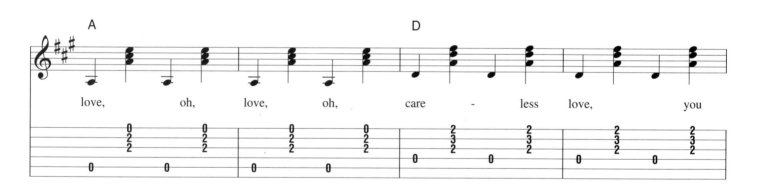

love,   oh,   love,   oh,   care - less   love,   you

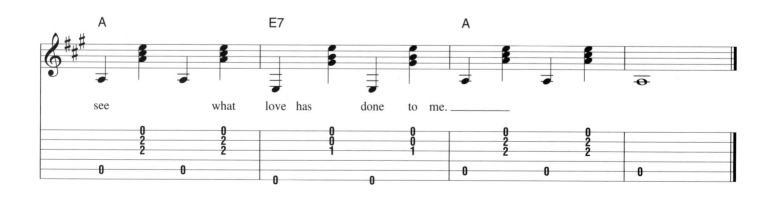

see   what   love has   done   to   me. _____

This next version of "Careless Love" contains a fingerpicking backup. To get started fingerpicking, play an A chord and position your picking hand as shown in the photo. You can also brace your picking hand by resting your ring and pinky fingers on the soundboard.

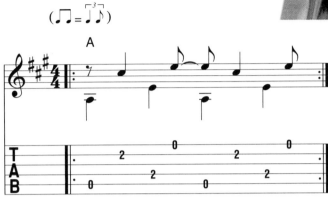

Pick the fifth string with your thumb, the second string with your index finger, the fourth string with your thumb, and the first string with your middle finger.

Repeat this four-note pattern over and over with the guitar on Track 24. Play the same pattern for the E7 chord, only change the first stroke so that your thumb picks the root note—the sixth string. The pattern is as follows: 6–2–4–1.

While playing the D chord, change the pattern so that your thumb plays the root note, D, like this:

Pick the fourth string with your thumb, the second string with your index finger, the third string with your thumb, and the first string with your middle finger.

This fingerpicking pattern is often referred to as an "alternating thumb" backup, as the thumb alternates between two bass notes, usually the root note and the 5th.

CARELESS LOVE
(KEY OF A MAJOR, ALTERNATING-THUMB BACKUP)

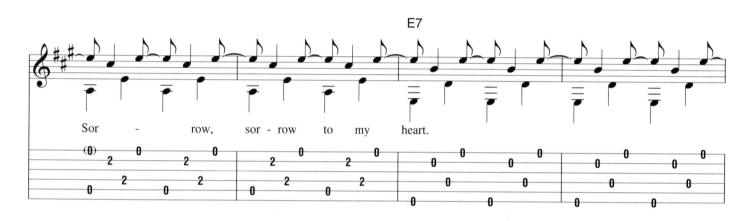

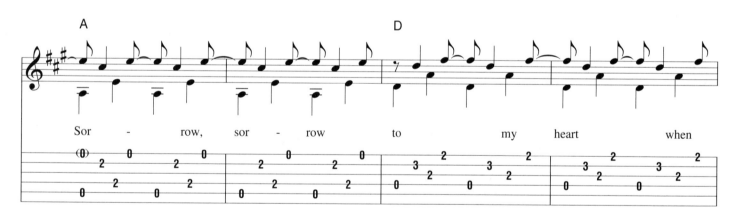

You can play "Careless Love" with a straight-eighths rock rhythm, as the next arrangement shows. As you did in "Straight-Eighths Blues Rock," from **ROADMAP #5**, strum eight downstrokes in each measure.

CARELESS LOVE
(KEY OF A MAJOR, ROCK GROOVE)

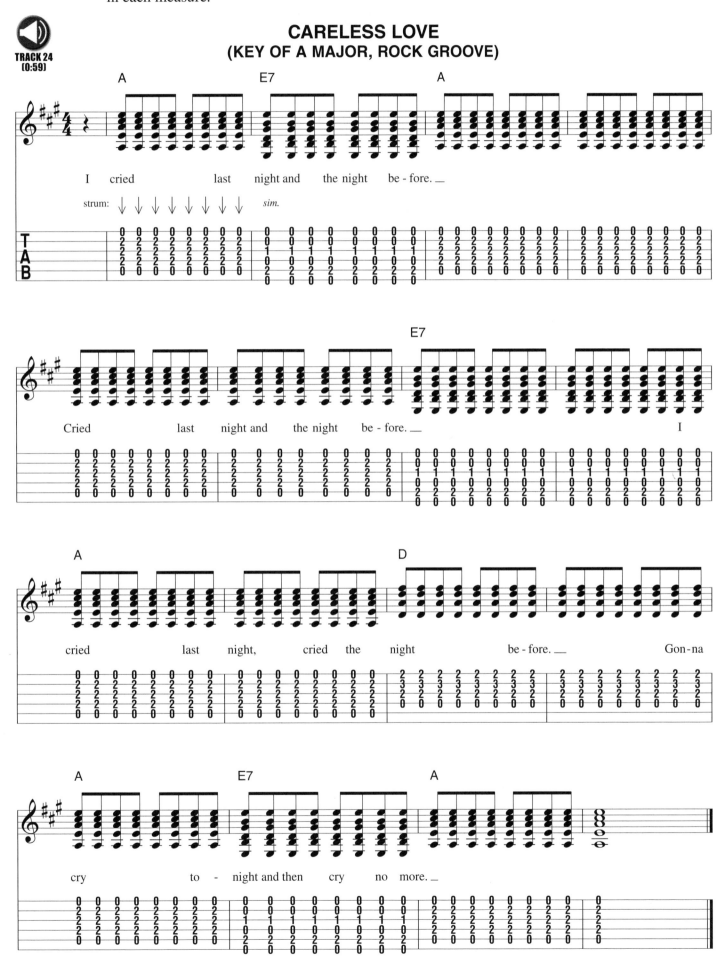

SUMMING UP—NOW YOU KNOW...

1. How to play A and E7 chords.

2. The I, IV, and V chords in the key of A major.

3. How to switch from one chord to another and strum a few songs in the key of A major.

4. How to play a basic fingerpicking, alternating-thumb backup pattern.

8

THE A MAJOR SCALE

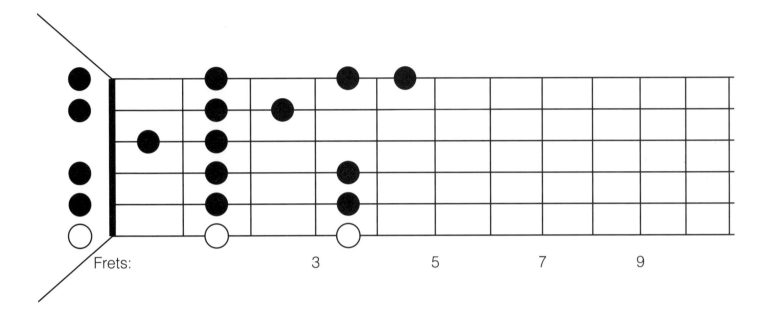

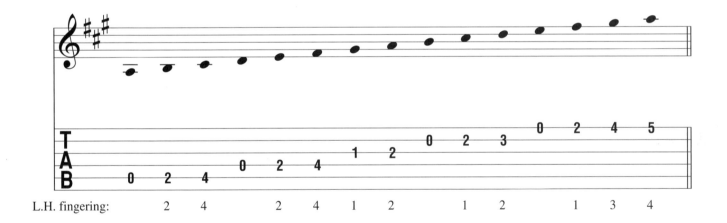

WHY? This scale enables you to play melodies in the key of A major.

WHAT? Like **ROADMAP #6**, **ROADMAP #8** is really two major scales, or two octaves of A major.

This Roadmap includes some "extra notes"—the white dots on the sixth string.

The A major scale contains the same notes as the D major scale, with one exception: The D scale includes a G natural (open third string and fret 3 of the first and sixth strings); the A scale contains a G♯ (fret 1 of the third string and fret 4 of the first and sixth strings).

HOW?

Practice two octaves of the A major scale over and over like this:

Now practice the lower octave of the A major scale and include the "extra notes."

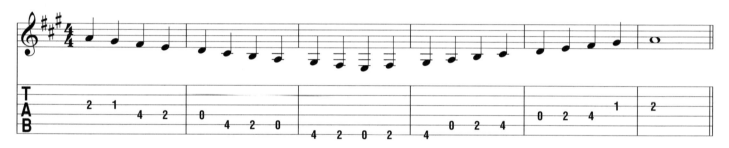

DO IT!

Try to play some melodies "by ear," using the A major scale.

Play "Careless Love," in the key of A major. It's written below, twice—first, in the lower octave, and then the higher octave.

CARELESS LOVE
(MELODY IN A MAJOR)

night and the night be - fore. I cried last night and the

night be - fore. Gon-na cry to - night, then cry no more.

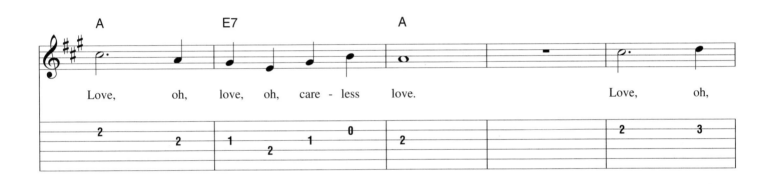

Love, oh, love, oh, care - less love. Love, oh,

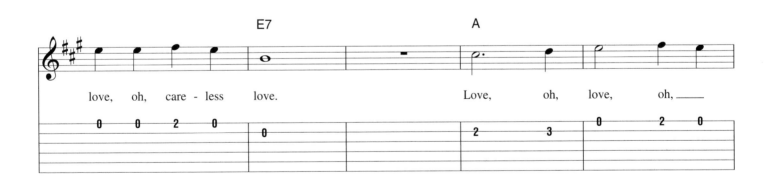

love, oh, care - less love. Love, oh, love, oh, ____

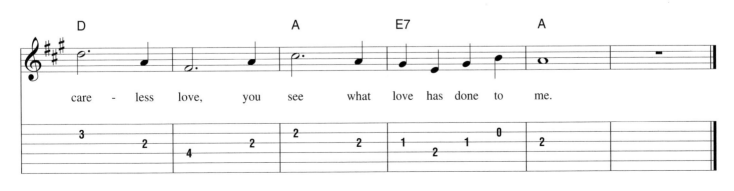

care - less love, you see what love has done to me.

Play the melody to "I Never Will Marry," in the key of A major.

I NEVER WILL MARRY
(MELODY IN A MAJOR)

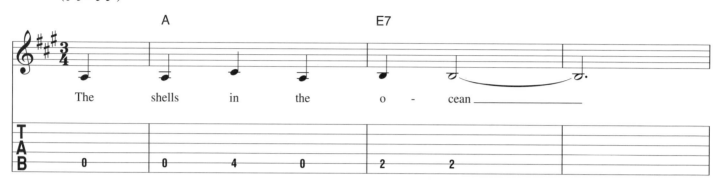

The shells in the o - cean

will ___ be my death - bed, ___

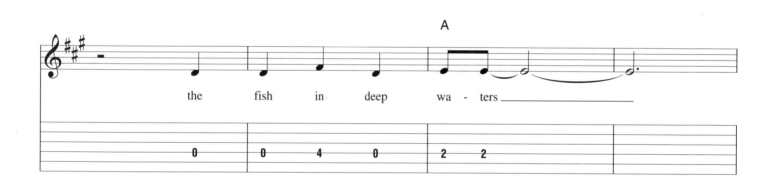

the fish in deep wa - ters ___

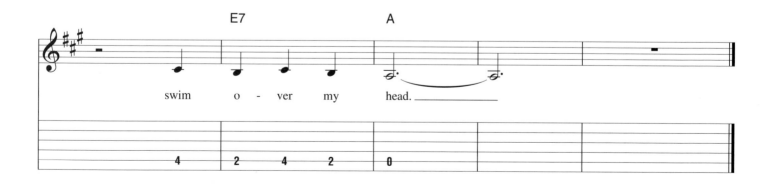

swim o - ver my head. ___

Now play "I Never Will Marry" flatpicking style (see **ROADMAP #6**), brushing down on the treble strings between the melody notes:

TRACK 27
[0:27]

I NEVER WILL MARRY
(MELODY IN A MAJOR, FLATPICKING STYLE)

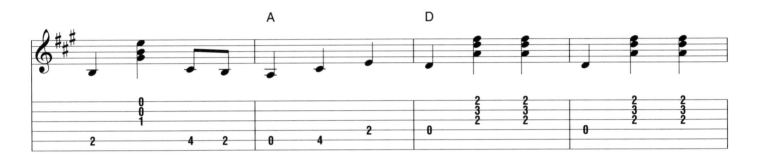

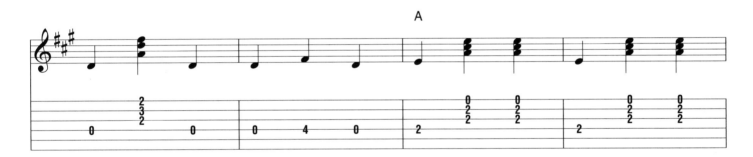

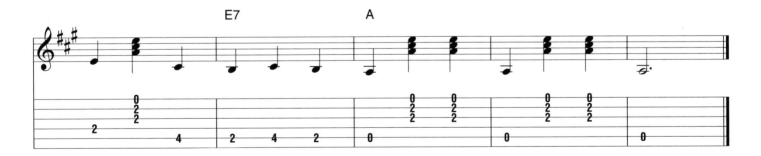

SUMMING UP—NOW YOU KNOW...

1. How to play the A major scale.
2. How to play a few familiar melodies in the key of A major.

9

THE C CHORD FAMILY

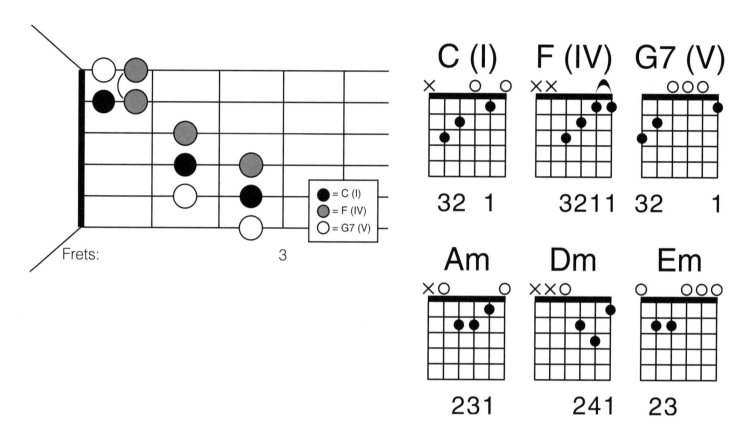

C (I) F (IV) G7 (V)

32 1 3211 32   1

Am Dm Em

231 241 23

● = C (I)
● = F (IV)
○ = G7 (V)

Frets: 3

WHY? With this chord family, you can play songs in the key of C major.

WHAT? In the key of C major, C is the I chord, F is the IV chord, and G7 is the V chord.

G7 contains only one note that differs from the G major chord. Try playing both the "easy," one-finger G7 and the "complete," three-finger G7, choosing whichever version works best for you.

TRACK 28
(0:00)

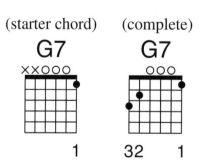

(starter chord) (complete)

G7 G7

1 32 1

F is a difficult chord; you have to flatten the index finger of your fretting hand to fret both the first and second strings. (This is called *barring.*) If it doesn't sound perfect, keep practicing! Your fretting hand will get stronger as the chord shape becomes more familiar.

The three minor chords written beneath **ROADMAP #9** are often used in songs in the key of C major. Every major chord has a *relative minor*—a closely related minor chord—and these are the three relative minors to the C chord family: Am is the relative minor to C, Dm to F, and Em to G. These minor chords will come in handy in other keys, as well. Notice how they resemble their major forms, especially Em and Am:

TRACK 28
(0:10)

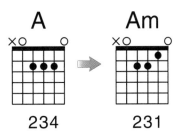

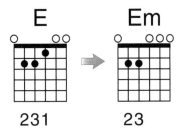

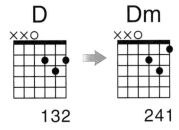

HOW? **Practice switching from C to G7 and from C to F, strumming in a steady tempo.** Notice that both are easy transitions, since your fretting hand keeps a similar position for all three chords:

TRACK 28
(0:28)

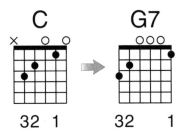

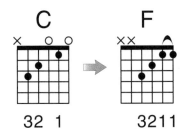

Practice switching from C to Am, from C to Dm, from G to Em, etc.

DO IT!   **Play "Careless Love" in the key of C major, using the flatpicking strum:**

TRACK 29

CARELESS LOVE
(KEY OF C MAJOR, FLATPICKING STYLE)

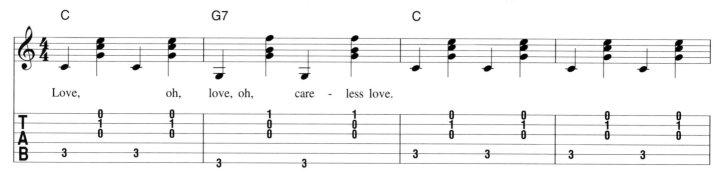

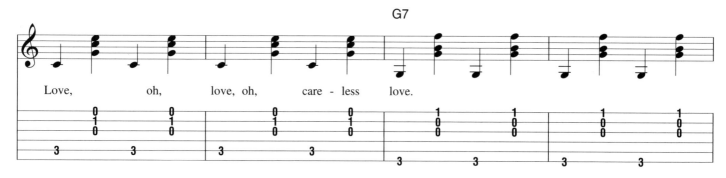

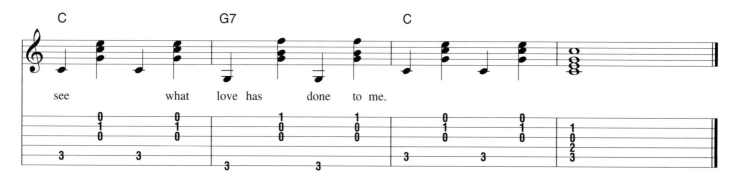

Play the folk tune "Sloop John B.," made popular by the Beach Boys on their *Pet Sounds* album, and most recently by Simple Minds. "Sloop John B." has a calypso feel, with a strum that also works for many rock, country rock, and folk rock tunes. This is the same strum that we used to play "Valley Rock" (Track 6).

TRACK 30
(0:00)

Here's a slightly fancier version of the same strum; just leave out the first upstroke. Your hand still strums eight strokes, but misses the strings on the first upstroke. It sounds like this:

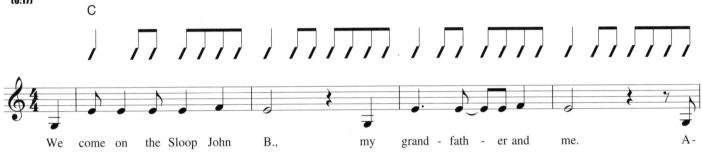

SLOOP JOHN B.
(KEY OF C MAJOR, FOLK-ROCK STRUM)

We come on the Sloop John B., my grand - fath - er and me. A-

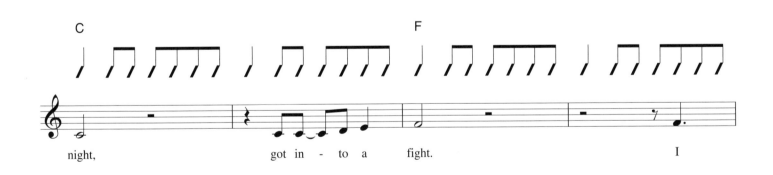

round Nas - sau town we ___ did roam. Drink - ing all

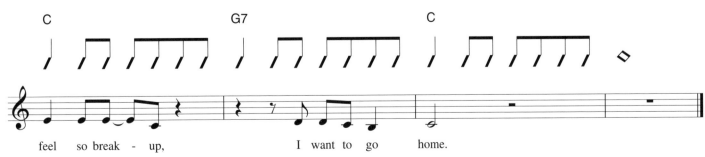

night, got in - to a fight. I

C — G7 — C

feel so break - up, I want to go home.

Play the folk song "The Water Is Wide" in the key of C major, using a slight variation of the "Sloop John B." calypso strum (miss the strings on the downstroke of beat 3, as shown below). This creates a more syncopated strum. The tune has been recorded by many jazz and pop artists, including Enya, James Taylor, Jewel, Sarah McLachlan, and more. It makes use of all three minor chords.

TRACK 31
(0:00)

TRACK 31
(0:10)

THE WATER IS WIDE
(KEY OF C MAJOR, FOLK-ROCK STRUM)

The wa-ter is wide, I can't get o - ver,

and nei - ther have I wings to fly.

Give me a boat that can car - ry two,

and both shall row, my love and I.

52

"St. James Infirmary Blues" makes use of two minor chords, as well as the E7 chord. This song has been recorded by countless blues artists, as well as the White Stripes, the Stray Cats, Van Morrison, and Mark Lanegan, among others. To get the slow shuffle-beat feel that you hear on Track 32, strum four downstrokes per measure, with an upstroke on the "and" of beat 3. The count is 1, 2, 3-&, 4:

ST. JAMES INFIRMARY BLUES
(KEY OF A MINOR, SLOW SHUFFLE-BEAT STRUM)

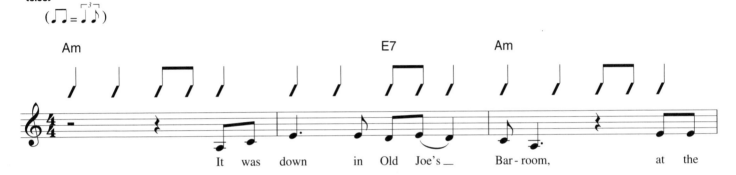

It was down in Old Joe's Bar-room, at the

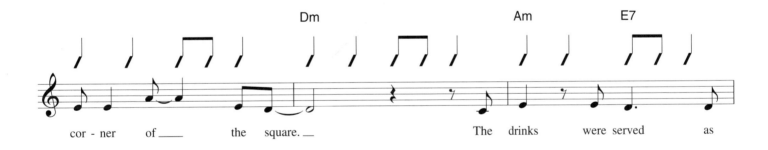

cor-ner of the square. The drinks were served as

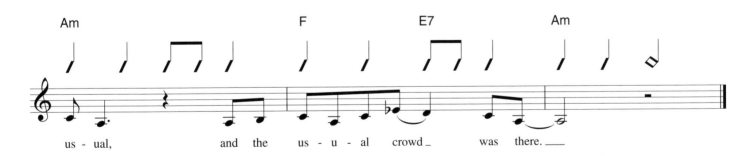

us-ual, and the us-u-al crowd was there.

"Rising Sun Blues" uses the C chord family (including Am), as well as the D and E7 chords. It's in 6/8 time, so use six down-strums per measure.

RISING SUN BLUES
(KEY OF A MINOR, 6/8 TIME STRUM)

TRACK 33
(0:08)

There is a house in New Or - leans _ that they call _____ the Ris - ing Sun, and it's been _____ the ru - in _____ of man-y a poor _ boy, _____ and God, I know _____ I'm one.

SUMMING UP—NOW YOU KNOW...

1. How to play F and G7 chords.

2. How to play three minor chords: Am, Dm, and Em.

3. The I, IV, and V chords in the key of C major.

4. How to switch from one chord to another and strum a few songs in the key of C major.

5. How to play a basic rock/calypso/folk strum.

6. How to play a slow shuffle-beat strum.

7. How to play a 6/8 time strum.

THE C MAJOR SCALE

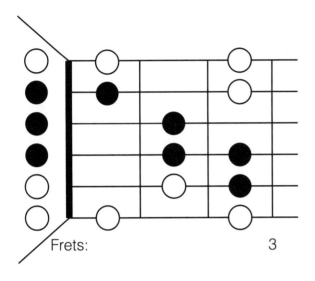

Frets: 3

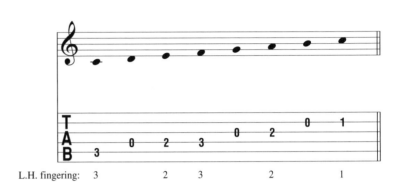

L.H. fingering: 3   2   3   2   1

WHY?   This scale will help you play melodies in the key of C major.

WHAT?   **"Extra notes" have been added above and below the C major scale,** similar to the other major scales that you've learned so far.

    The C major scale contains the same notes as the G major scale, with one exception: The G major scale includes an F♯ (fret 4 of the fourth string and fret 2 of the first and sixth strings). The C major scale has an F natural, which is one fret lower than F♯.

HOW?   **Practice the C major scale as it's written in notation and tablature in ROADMAP #10,** then play it with the "extra notes" (white dots), over and over:

TRACK 34

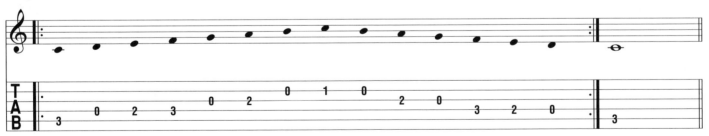

DO IT! Try to play a few melodies "by ear," using the C major scale.

Play the melody to "Sloop John B." in the key of C major, in both a low and a high register:

TRACK 35

SLOOP JOHN B.
(MELODY IN C MAJOR)

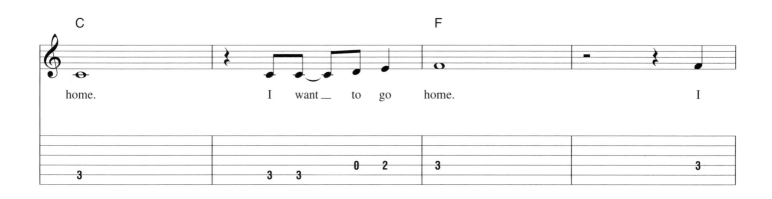

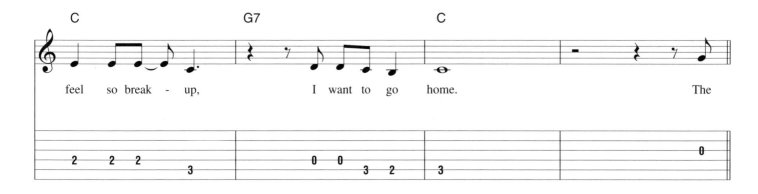

56

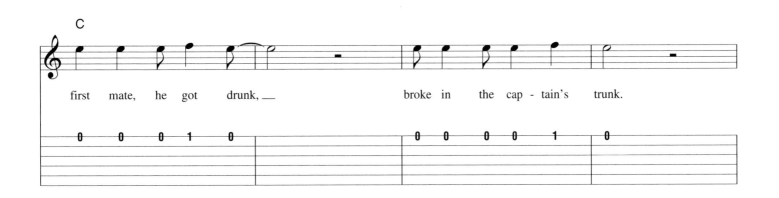

first mate, he got drunk, __ broke in the cap - tain's trunk.

Con - sta - ble had to come and take __ him a - way. Sher - iff John

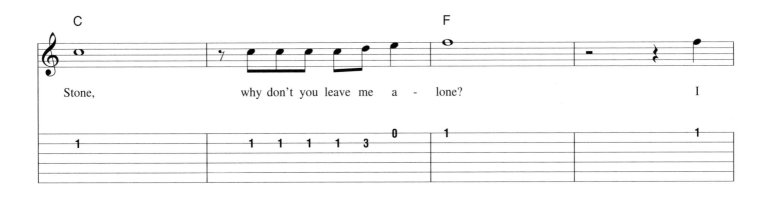

Stone, why don't you leave me a - lone? I

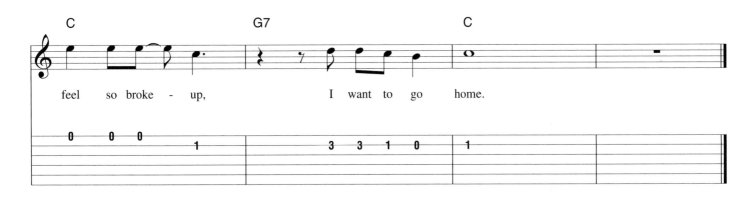

feel so broke - up, I want to go home.

Do the same with "The Water Is Wide."

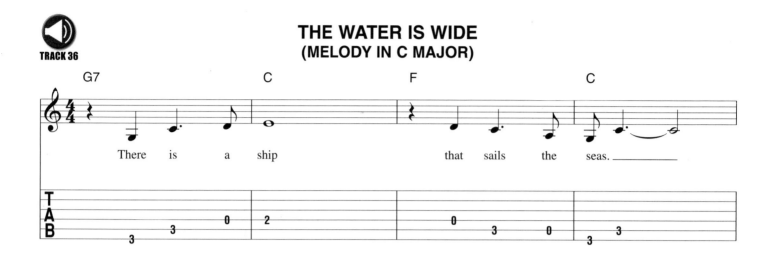

THE WATER IS WIDE
(MELODY IN C MAJOR)

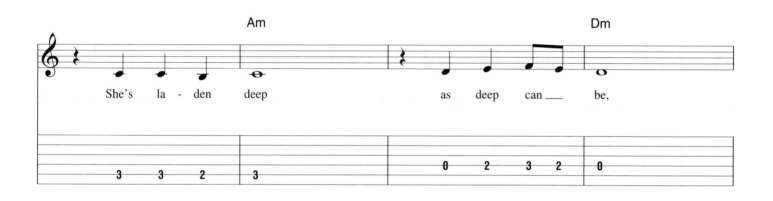

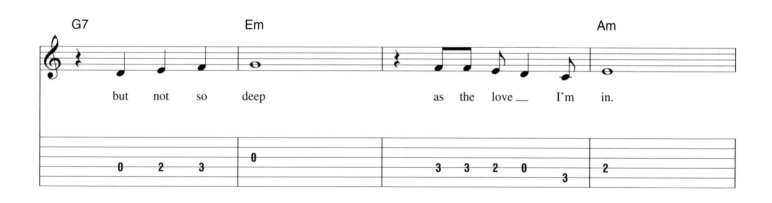

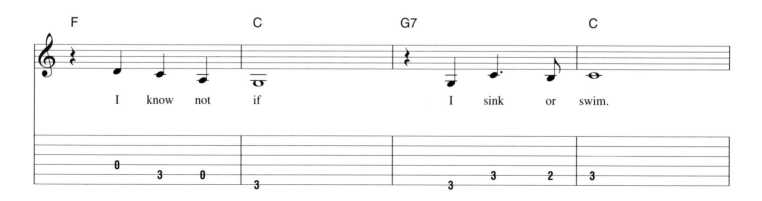

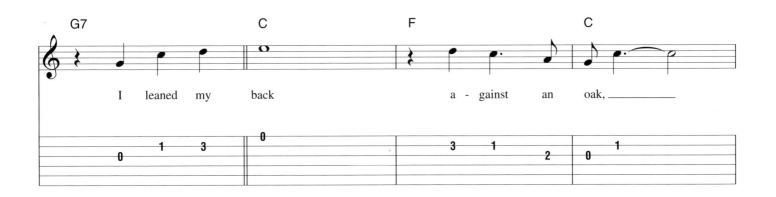

I leaned my back a - gainst an oak, _____

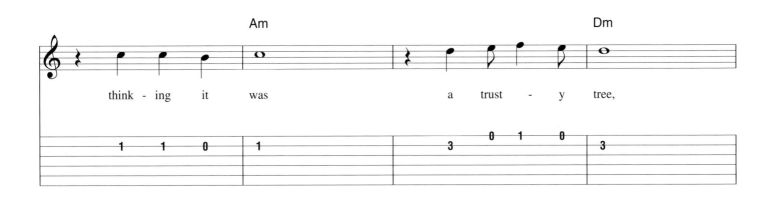

think - ing it was a trust - y tree,

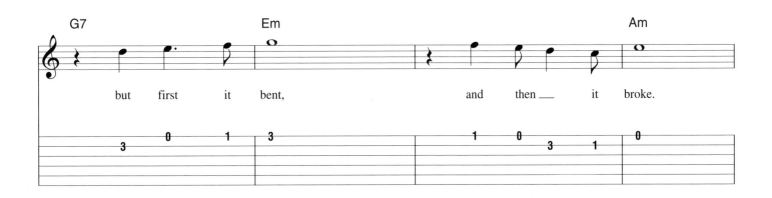

but first it bent, and then ___ it broke.

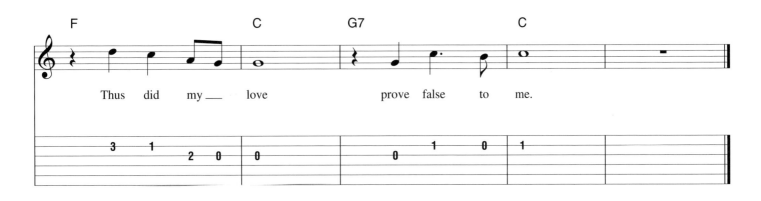

Thus did my ___ love prove false to me.

Play the melody to "St. James Infirmary Blues" in two registers. The song is in the key of A minor, and its melody is composed of notes from the C major scale.

Every major chord has a "relative minor," a minor chord that is a very close relative to and shares scale notes with the major chord. Am is the relative minor of C.

You may notice that one note that appears in this melody is not in the C major scale: E♭ (E-flat). The E♭ note is a "blue note," a flatted 3rd. Blues songs like "St. James Infirmary Blues" often include ♭3rds and ♭7ths, and sometimes ♭5ths, as well. These notes help to make the melodies sound bluesy.

ST. JAMES INFIRMARY BLUES
(MELODY IN A MINOR)

SUMMING UP—NOW YOU KNOW...

1. How to play a C major scale.

2. How to play a few familiar melodies in the keys of C major and A minor.

3. The meaning of the terms "relative minor" and "blue note."

THE E CHORD FAMILY

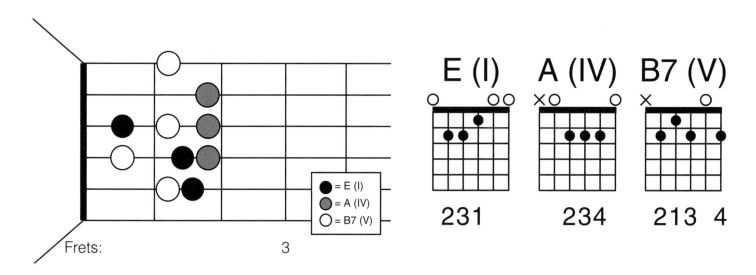

E (I) A (IV) B7 (V)

231   234   213 4

= E (I)
= A (IV)
= B7 (V)

Frets: 3

WHY? These chords enable you to play songs in the key of E major.

WHAT? In the key of E major, E is the I chord, A is the IV chord, and B7 is the V chord.

The E chord differs from E7 by one note:

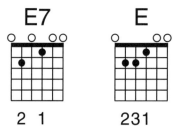

E7   E

2 1   231

TRACK 38

HOW? **Practice switching from E to B7 and from E to A.** For both E and B7, your middle finger frets the fifth string at fret 2, so keep the fifth string fretted as you change from E to B7 and back.

If you use the suggested fingerings, both your middle finger and your ring finger move up a string when changing from E to A:

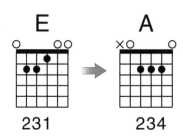

E   A

231   234

DO IT! **Play "The Midnight Special" in the key of E major.** This prison song, popularized by Leadbelly, has been recorded by a long list of blues, folk, R&B, and rock artists. In this version, you'll play the Carter strum, but take it a step further—play a "brush-up" after the "brush-down" on the treble strings on the "ands" of beats 2 and 4. Here's the pattern, using an E chord:

TRACK 39
(0:00)

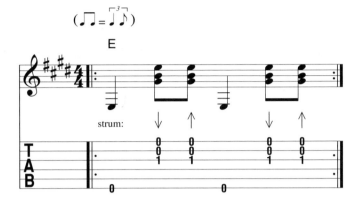

Pick the bottom (sixth) string with your thumb or a flat pick; brush down and up on the high strings (strings 3–1) with your index finger or the pick.

Do the same on the A and B7 chords, but pick the fifth string instead of the sixth.

THE MIDNIGHT SPECIAL
(KEY OF E MAJOR, FLATPICKING STYLE)

TRACK 39
(0:07)

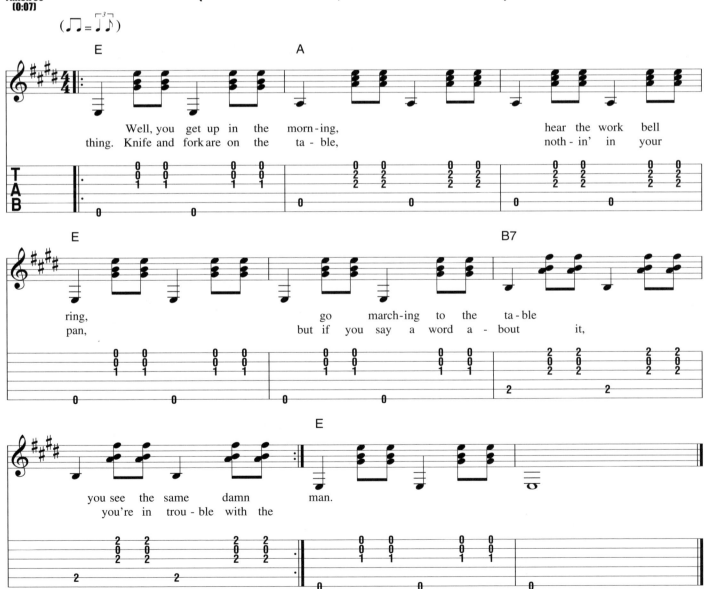

Play "Stagolee" in the key of E major. This old blues tune has been a hit on pop, R&B, blues, and country charts. This version makes use of the "alternating-thumb" fingerpicking pattern that you used for "Careless Love" (Track 24).

TRACK 40

STAGOLEE
(KEY OF E MAJOR, ALTERNATING-THUMB BACKUP)

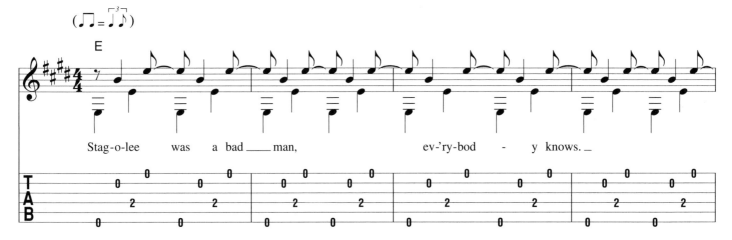

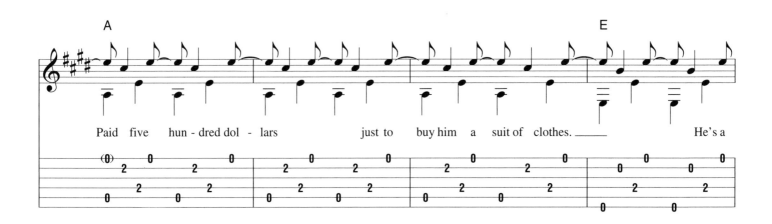

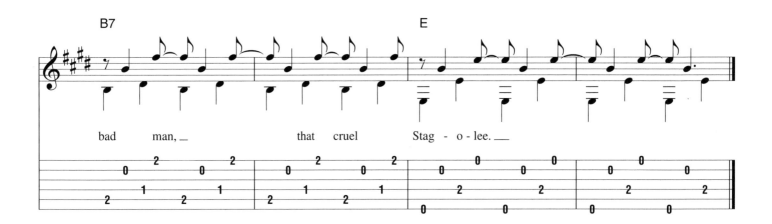

Play the western ballad "Streets of Laredo" in the key of E major. It's a waltz (3/4 time), but instead of using the flatpicking waltz strum, this arrangement involves fingerpicking. Play an E chord using the six-step pattern on the next page.

Here is the fingerpicking sequence:

- Pick the sixth string with your thumb (t)
- Pick the third string with your index finger (i)
- Pick the second string with your middle finger (m)
- Pick the first string with your ring finger (r)
- Pick the second string with your middle finger
- Pick the third string with your index finger

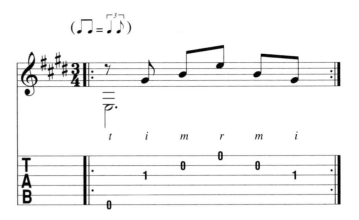

Play the same pattern for both the A chord and the B7 chord, but start on the fifth string for both (to play the root note, or the note that gives the chord its name).

STREETS OF LAREDO
(KEY OF E MAJOR, FINGERPICKING 3/4 TIME)

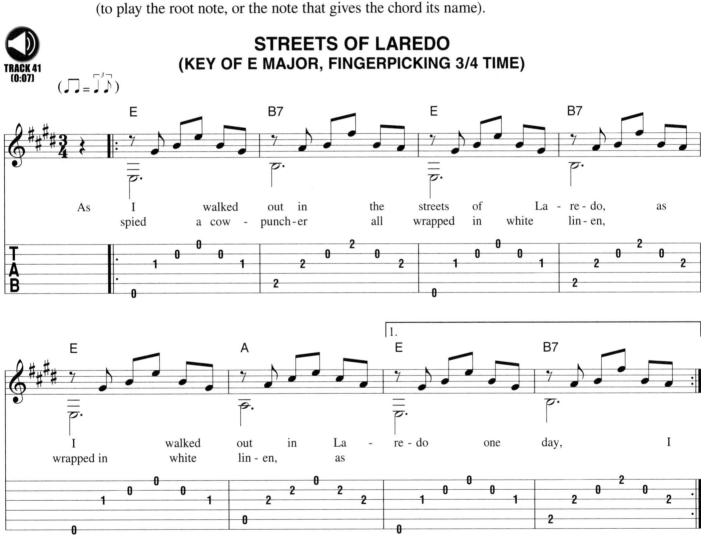

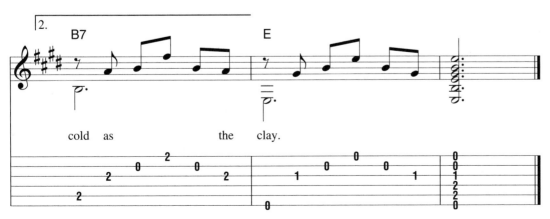

You can use this same six-note fingerpicking pattern to play in 6/8 time, which has six beats per measure (see How to Read Music, page 89). By slightly altering the timing, it also works for "Rising Sun Blues" (Track 33):

RISING SUN BLUES
(KEY OF A MINOR, FINGERPICKING 6/8 TIME)

Many blues guitarists—electric and acoustic—favor the key of E major. One reason is the popular two-string boogie backup, which is easy to play in this key. Your thumb or flat pick brushes down on two bass notes simultaneously—the sixth and fifth strings or the fifth and fourth strings, as shown on the next page. The odd B7 chord (or the "lazy person's" B7) is a trademark of the great bluesman Jimmy Reed, who was a big influence on the Rolling Stones and many other rock and blues artists.

The two-note versions of the E and A chords are called E5 and A5 because they include only the root and 5th of the chords. Also known as *power chords*, you'll learn more about them in **ROADMAP #15**.

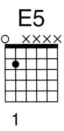

E5

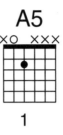

A5

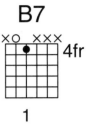

B7

To play the boogie lick on the E chord, strum down on the two lowest bass notes, and alternate fretting the fifth string at the second and the fourth frets. Fret the second fret with your index finger and the fourth fret with your ring finger.

TRACK 43
(0:00)

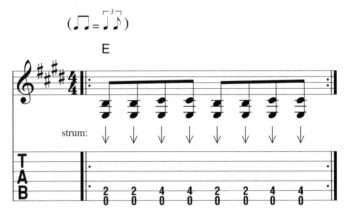

The A lick is just like the E lick, moved up one string:

TRACK 43
(0:06)

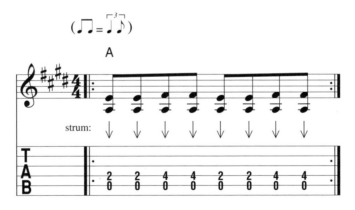

The B7 lick is just like the A lick, moved up two frets:

TRACK 43
(0:12)

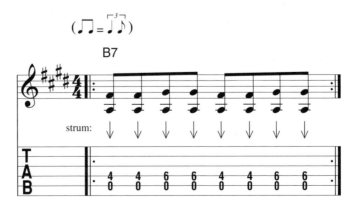

This conventional 12-bar blues demonstrates how to use the boogie-backup lick:

12-BAR BLUES
(BOOGIE BACKUP)

TRACK 43
[0:20]

Goin' a-way, ba-by, I won't be back 'til fall. ___ I'm

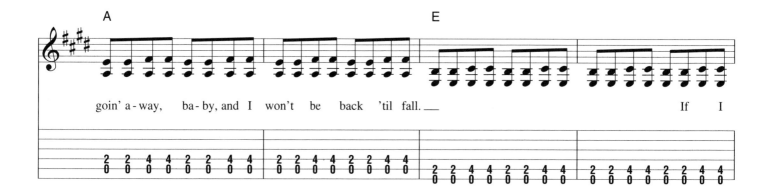

goin' a-way, ba-by, and I won't be back 'til fall. ___ If I

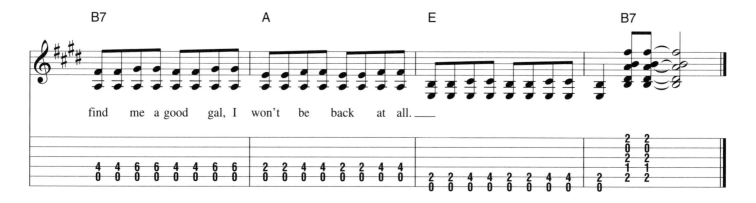

find me a good gal, I won't be back at all. ___

SUMMING UP—NOW YOU KNOW...

1. How to play E and B7 chords.

2. The I, IV, and V chords in the key of E major.

3. How to switch from one chord to another and strum a few songs in the key of E major.

4. A fingerpicking pattern for 3/4 and 6/8 time.

5. How to play a boogie-backup lick on the bass strings that is used in 12-bar blues, rock, and in R&B tunes.

THE E MAJOR SCALE

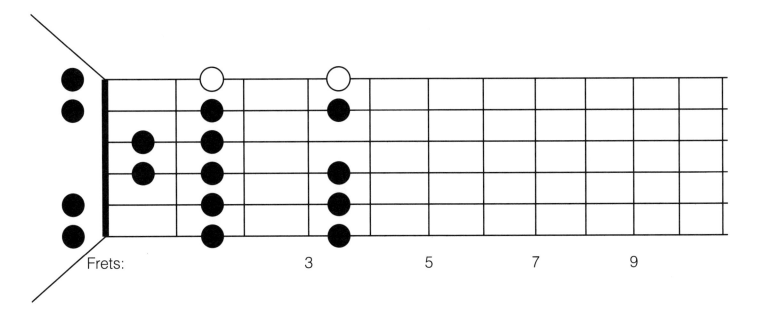

Frets: 3   5   7   9

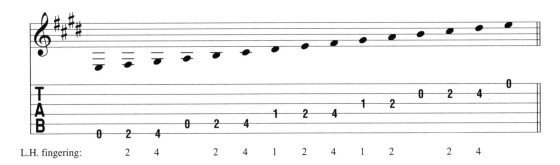

L.H. fingering: 2   4   2   4   1   2   4   1   2   2   4

WHY? With this scale, you can play melodies in the key of E major.

WHAT? **ROADMAP #12 shows you how to play a two-octave E major scale** with a few extra notes in the high register (the white dots).

The E major scale contains the same notes as the A major scale, with one exception: The A major scale includes a D natural (open fourth string and fret 3 of the second string); the E major scale contains a D♯, one fret higher than D natural.

HOW?

TRACK 44

Practice each octave of the E major scale over and over, and then combine them in a loop with the extra notes:

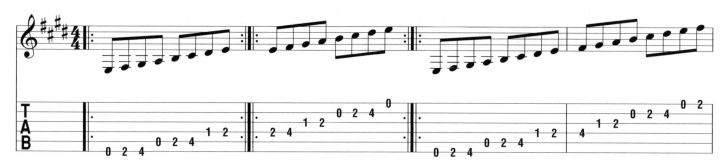

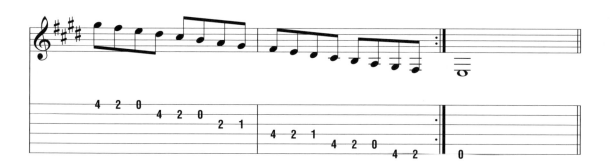

DO IT!

Try to play a few melodies "by ear" using the E major scale.

Play the melody to "Streets of Laredo" in the key of E major:

STREETS OF LAREDO
(MELODY IN E MAJOR)

TRACK 45

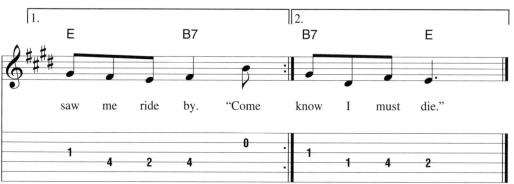

Play the melody to "The Midnight Special" in the key of E major, in two registers:

THE MIDNIGHT SPECIAL
(MELODY IN E MAJOR)

TRACK 47
[0:00]

Play the melody to "When the Saints Go Marching In" in the key of E major. Two versions of the tune are written below. The first is the melody, and the second is a flatpicking-style arrangement in which you fill out the rhythm with brush strokes on the treble strings (à la "Wildwood Flower," Track 20) between breaks in the melody. This time, every downstroke on the treble strings is immediately followed by an upstroke, which gives the tune a fuller sound:

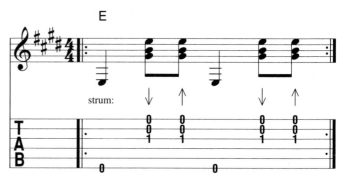

TRACK 47
[0:05]

WHEN THE SAINTS GO MARCHING IN
(MELODY IN E MAJOR)

72

Carter-style…

SUMMING UP—NOW YOU KNOW...

1. How to play the E major scale.

2. How to play a few familiar melodies in the key of E major.

3. How to embellish a melody with a fuller flatpicking strum, which includes down- and upstrokes.

NOTES ON THE FRETBOARD

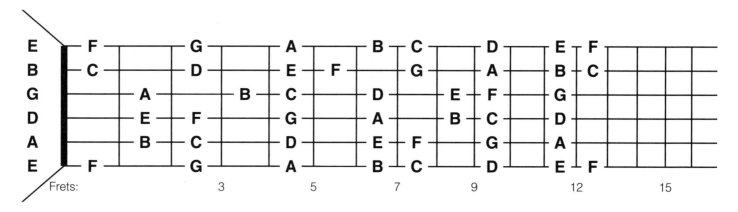

It's helpful, for many reasons, to know some—or all—of the notes on the fretboard. For example, to make use of the next two chapters (**ROADMAP #14** and **ROADMAP #15**), you need to know the notes on the fifth and sixth strings. As you progress on the guitar, you may want to know the names of the notes in the chords that you're playing to understand chord construction. Knowing the names of notes helps you communicate with other players and enables you to learn to read music.

WHAT? As you go up the alphabet and up the fretboard, the notes get higher in pitch.

A whole step is two frets; a half step is one fret. Most notes are a whole step apart (e.g., D is two frets above C, E is two frets above D), but half steps (one fret) appear in two places: from B to C and from E to F.

Sharps are one fret higher: sixth string/fret 3 = G, so sixth string/fret 4 = G♯; sixth string/fret 8 = C, so sixth string/fret 9 = C♯.

Flats are one fret lower: sixth string/fret 5 = A, so sixth string/fret 4 = A♭; sixth string/fret 10 = D, so sixth string/fret 9 = D♭.

Some notes have two names. Sixth string/fret 4 is both G♯ and A♭. The name you use depends on the musical context.

HOW? Fretboard markings help. Most guitars have fretboard inlays or marks somewhere on the neck, indicating the third, fifth, seventh, ninth, and 12th frets. Be aware of these signposts—once you have memorized the fact that fret 5 of the sixth string is an A note, the fifth-fret fretboard mark helps you get there fast.

Everything starts over at the 12th fret. The 12th fret is like a second nut. On the sixth string, three frets above the nut, is a G note; three frets above the 12th fret (again, on the sixth string) is also a G. In other words, the 12th fret is an octave higher than the open strings.

The sixth and first strings are the same. When you memorize the sixth-string notes, you also have memorized the first-string notes.

DO IT!

Start by memorizing the notes on the sixth and fifth strings. You will need to know these notes very soon—for **ROADMAP #14** and **ROADMAP #15**.

Walk up the sixth string, naming the notes as you go. Start with the letter names (F, G, etc.); add the sharps and/or flats later.

Spot-check yourself on the sixth string. Play random notes, out of order, naming them as they're played.

Learn the fifth-string notes the same way: Walk up the string, naming the notes, then spot-check yourself by playing random notes.

Play sixth- and fourth-string octave shapes to learn the fourth-string notes. When you use the hand position shown below to play the sixth and fourth strings simultaneously, the fourth-string note is the same note as the one on the sixth string, only it's an octave (eight notes) higher. Once you have memorized the notes on the sixth string, this method is a shortcut to learning the fourth-string notes.

Two G notes:

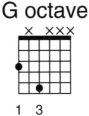

G octave

After playing a lot of octaves, walk up the fourth string, naming the notes as you go and using the sixth string as a reference point. Then spot-check yourself on the fourth string, using the same method that you used on the sixth string.

Play fifth- and third-string octaves to learn the third-string notes. That way, you can reference the third-string notes with the fifth-string notes:

Two C notes:

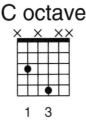

C octave

Walk up the second string, naming the notes as you go. Then play random notes on the second string, naming them as they're played.

SUMMING UP—NOW YOU KNOW...

1. The location of the notes on the fretboard, especially on the fifth and sixth strings.
2. Helpful shortcuts for memorizing the notes on the fretboard.
3. The meaning of these musical terms: sharp, flat, whole step, half step.

THE MOVEABLE BLUES BOX

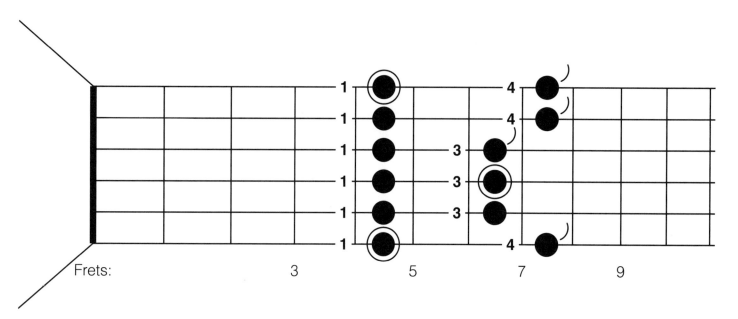

WHY? The moveable blues box is a universal jamming tool! It will help you play melodies and improvise licks and solos in any key, in any genre: blues, rock, country, jazz, folk, or bluegrass.

WHAT? **ROADMAP #14** is an A minor pentatonic (five-note) scale. It's sometimes called the "blues box" because the notes are in a box-like configuration on the fretboard.

TRACK 48
(0:00)

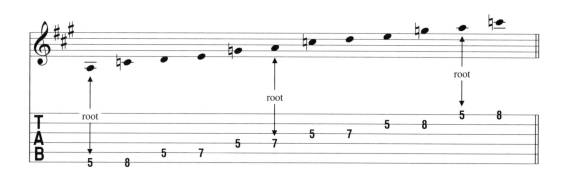

You can use the minor pentatonic scale (the blues box) to solo in a minor or a major key. For example, the A blues box shown in **ROADMAP #14** works as a soloing device whether a tune is in the key of A, or the key of A minor.

The blues box is moveable, since it includes no unfretted strings. If you move it down two frets so that it begins at the third fret, it's now a G minor pentatonic scale, instead of an A minor pentatonic scale. If you start at the first fret, it's an F minor pentatonic scale.

The roots are circled. Use the first or sixth string as a guide to place the blues box in the appropriate key. To play in the key of C, begin the scale at fret 8 of the sixth string, because fret 8 of the sixth string is a C note.

Unlike the major scale, the minor pentatonic scale has only five notes: 1–♭3–4–5–♭7. It lends itself to blues or blues-tinged melodies, solos, and licks and is the basis of electric blues and blues rock soloing, although it can be played on an acoustic guitar, as well.

Often, you can stay in one blues position and play licks and melodies throughout an entire tune, in spite of the chord changes that occur in the tune. If a song is in the key of A, use the A blues box shown in **ROADMAP #14**. This approach makes soloing easy, once you know how to use the scale to create licks and phrases.

The numbers in **ROADMAP #14** are suggested left-hand fingerings. The scale notes with small, curved lines can be bent ("stretched" or "choked"). This left-hand technique, described below, is important to the blues sound.

HOW? The F chord you learned in **ROADMAP #9** can be played all over the fretboard, as long as you only strum the fretted strings and avoid the open (sixth and fifth) strings. For example, if you play it a fret higher than usual, it's an F# chord. When played anywhere other than the first fret, it's called an F formation, and it's a very useful formation for playing the blues! The sixth and/or first string is the root of the F formation. If played at the fifth fret, it's an A chord, because the first string and the sixth string are both A notes.

To put your left hand in position for the first blues box, fret an F-chord formation at the fret that matches your key, using the sixth string as a guide. For instance, the note at fret 5 of the sixth string is an A, so, for the key of A, play an F-chord formation at fret 5. You'll be playing an A chord and your hand will be in position for the A blues box. You don't have to maintain the F-chord formation while playing the scale, but it is a helpful reference point and contains a high (first-string) and low (fourth-string) root note.

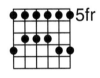
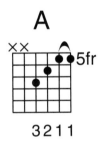

A

3 2 1 1

To bend (or "choke") a string, push it up or pull it down with your fretting finger (see photo). This raises the string's pitch one, two, or three frets higher than usual. You can control the pitch change by bending or releasing the string, making a note swoop or glide (as heard on Track 48). Bending strings is an important element in blues guitar, as well as in rock and country.

TRACK 48
(0:06)

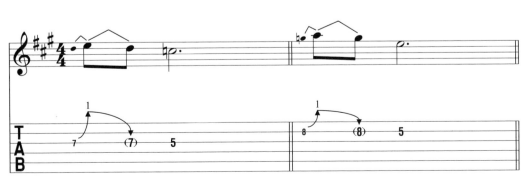

Some other great expressive soloing techniques are *hammer-ons* **and** *pull-offs,* indicated by the curved lines in the examples below (measures 3 and 5). For the hammer-on, you pick the first note and then fret the note above it without picking it. Hit, or hammer, the note hard enough to make it sound with your fretting hand alone. The pull-off is the reverse of this idea. Pick the first note and then pull your fret-hand finger off the string with a plucking motion, so it sounds the fretted note or open string below it.

TRACK 48
(0:13)

DO IT!

Once you've practiced the scale and blues licks, use the blues box to find the melodies to popular blues and rock tunes, such as: "Black Magic Woman," "Evil Ways," "Route 66," "Hound Dog," "The Thrill Is Gone," "Stormy Monday," and "Baby, Please Don't Go."

Play the blues tune "C.C. Rider" in the key of A major. The melody, which is played with the A blues box, resembles "Shake, Rattle, and Roll" and many other popular R&B tunes. It's a 12-bar blues, like Track 43.

TRACK 49

C.C. RIDER
(MELODY IN A MAJOR)

C.   C.   rid - er,   see _____ what   you _ have   done. _

C.   C.   rid - er,   see _____ what   you _ have   done. _   You

made me love you, now _____ your man _ has come. _

You can use the blues box to improvise (or "jam"). "Generic Rock" is a conventional rock progression in the key of C major. The lead guitar solo is an ad lib based on the C blues box.

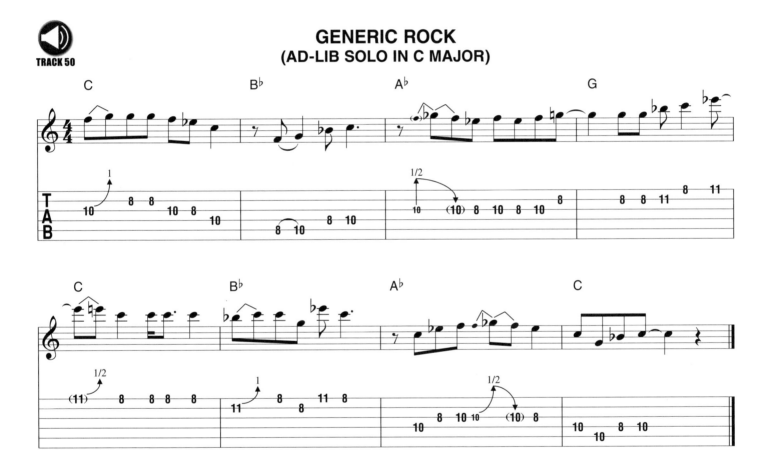

GENERIC ROCK
(AD-LIB SOLO IN C MAJOR)

TRACK 50

You can use the blues box to solo on any tune—even one that doesn't have a blues flavor. If a song's melody is based on the major scale, with few—or no—blue notes, blues box-based soloing may clash and sound inappropriate. In these tunes, a soloist can **use the blues box that is three frets below the actual key.**

For example, the folk ballad "Chilly Winds" is in the key of C major. If you try to play C blues box licks along with it (at fret 8), they'll clash. But, if you move the C blues box down three frets, to fret 5, it works fine. The reason for this is rather complicated (it has to do with relative minors, mentioned in the **ROADMAP #9** chapter), but the rule is simple: **If the blues box doesn't sound right with a tune, move it down three frets!** On the next page, listen to the lead guitar in "Chilly Winds," and then play the solo.

CHILLY WINDS
(KEY OF C MAJOR, AD-LIB SOLO WITH A BLUES BOX)

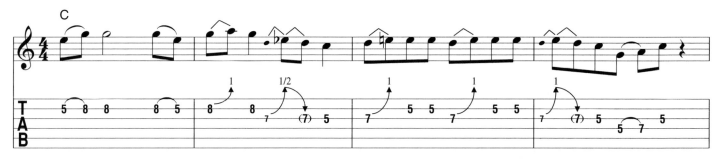

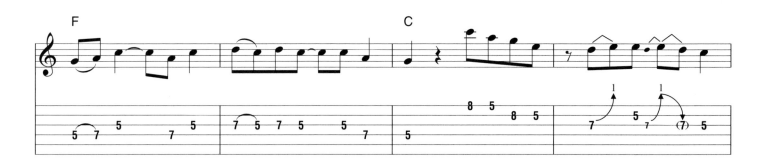

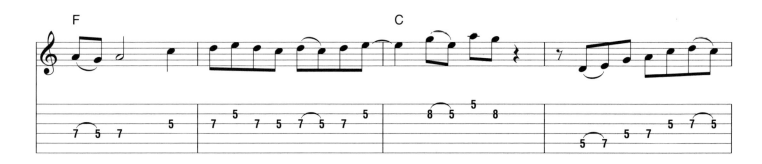

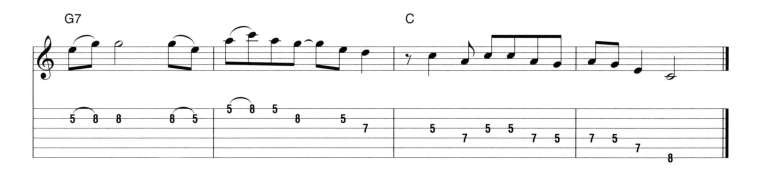

SUMMING UP—NOW YOU KNOW...

1. The notes of the minor pentatonic scale.

2. How to play the minor pentatonic scale (or "blues box") in any key.

3. How to bend (or "choke") a string.

4. The hammer-on and pull-off techniques.

5. How to play a few bluesy licks in any key and create an ad-lib solo.

6. How to use the blues box to solo, even when a song is not a blues.

BARRE CHORDS & POWER CHORDS

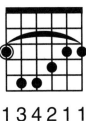 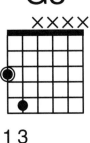 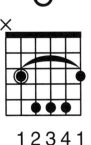 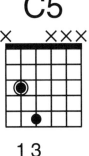

G   G5   C   C5

1 3 4 2 1 1   1 3   1 2 3 4 1   1 3

● = root

WHY? If you can play barre chords and power chords, you can play in any key, all over the fretboard. Knowing how to play these chords greatly expands your chord vocabulary and versatility. (Note: Many beginners find barre chords difficult. While practicing them will strengthen your hands, if they feel impossible at first, start with the power chords, as they're played with just two fingers and are fairly easy, even for beginners.)

WHAT? **The barred E-chord shape is an E major chord formation with a *barre* behind it.** (The "barre" is the index finger, flattened over all six strings.) The barre chord is moveable; you can play it at various frets to create different major chords.

E   barred E shape

2 3 1   1 3 4 2 1 1

The *power chord* grew out of the popular E blues boogie-backup style that you played in "12-Bar Blues" (Track 43). But moveable power chords can be played in any key, all over the fretboard. The power chord is usually named with a "5" (such as "G5"), which indicates that the chord contains the root note (G) and the 5th note (D) of the G major scale.

The sixth- and fifth-string power chord is a two-finger, moveable version of the E chord used in "12-Bar Blues." It's also a simplified version of the barred E shape:

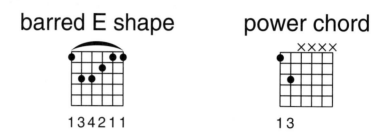

The barred A-chord formation is an A major chord shape with a barre behind it. To form this chord, the index finger barres five strings:

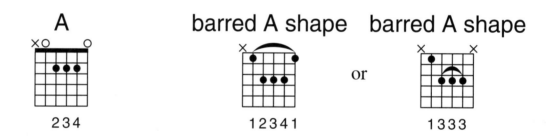

The fifth- and fourth-string power chord is a two-finger, simplified A-chord shape. It's a moveable version of the A chord used in "12-Bar Blues."

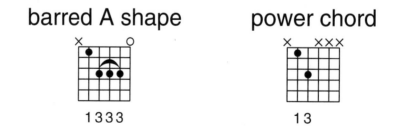

Power chords are often used for accompaniment (or "backup") in rock, blues, R&B, and country music.

HOW? **The sixth string is the root of the barred E-chord shape (the note that gives the chord its name).** To place the chord where you want it, find the appropriate note on the sixth string. For example, to play a C chord, fret the barred E-chord formation at fret 8, which, on the sixth string, is a C note.

C	A	G	F
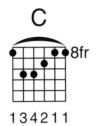	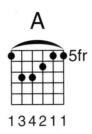		
1 3 4 2 1 1	1 3 4 2 1 1	1 3 4 2 1 1	1 3 4 2 1 1

The same goes for the sixth- and fifth-string power chord. The sixth string is its root, so reference the sixth string to find your power chord's root note.

C5	A5	G5	F5
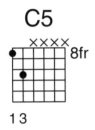	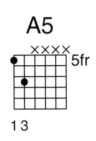	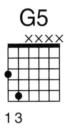	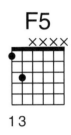
1 3	1 3	1 3	1 3

The fifth string is the root of the barred A-chord shape. To find the appropriate place to play your fifth-string barre chord, simply find its root note on the fifth string. For example, to play a C chord, fret the barred A-chord formation at fret 3, which, on the fifth string, is a C note.

C	D	E	F
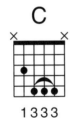	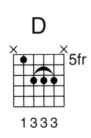	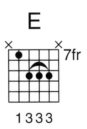	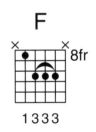
1 3 3 3	1 3 3 3	1 3 3 3	1 3 3 3

The same goes for the fifth- and fourth-string power chord. The fifth string is its root, so reference the fifth string to find your power chord's root note.

C5	D5	E5	F5
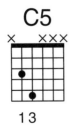	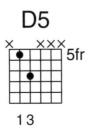	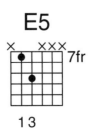	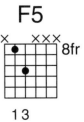
1 3	1 3	1 3	1 3

DO IT! With moveable power chords, you can play boogie backup licks in any key. Here's "C.C. Rider" again, played in A this time, using power chords.

C.C. RIDER
(KEY OF A MAJOR, WITH MOVEABLE BOOGIE BACKUP)

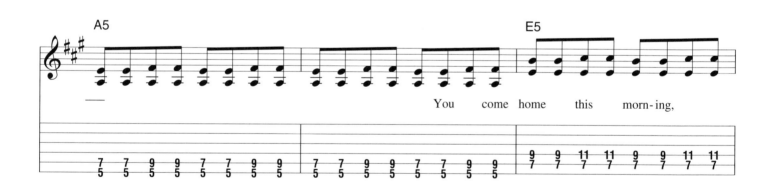

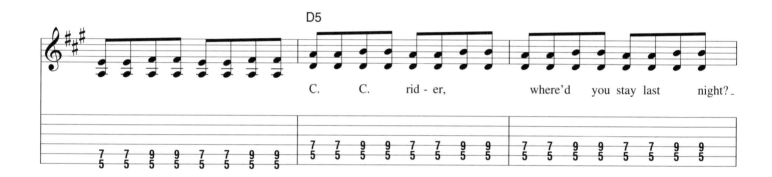

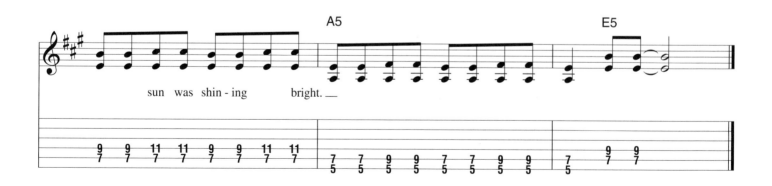

Power chords (with or without the boogie lick) are used in many rock riffs, as well as in entire chord progressions. "Classic Rock Progression," below, is an example:

CLASSIC ROCK PROGRESSION
(KEY OF G MAJOR, WITH POWER CHORDS)

*Strike chord on repeat.

The two moveable barre-chord shapes of ROADMAP #15 can be altered slightly to produce seventh chords and minor chords. This triples your chord vocabulary!

Change the barred E chord shape to a minor or seventh shape, the same way you changed E to E7 or Em:

Change the barred A chord shape to a minor or seventh shape the same way you changed A to A7 or Am:

Like the major barre chords, the barred minor chords and seventh chords are located by their fifth- and sixth-string roots. The following rendition of the centuries-old tune "Greensleeves" uses many of them:

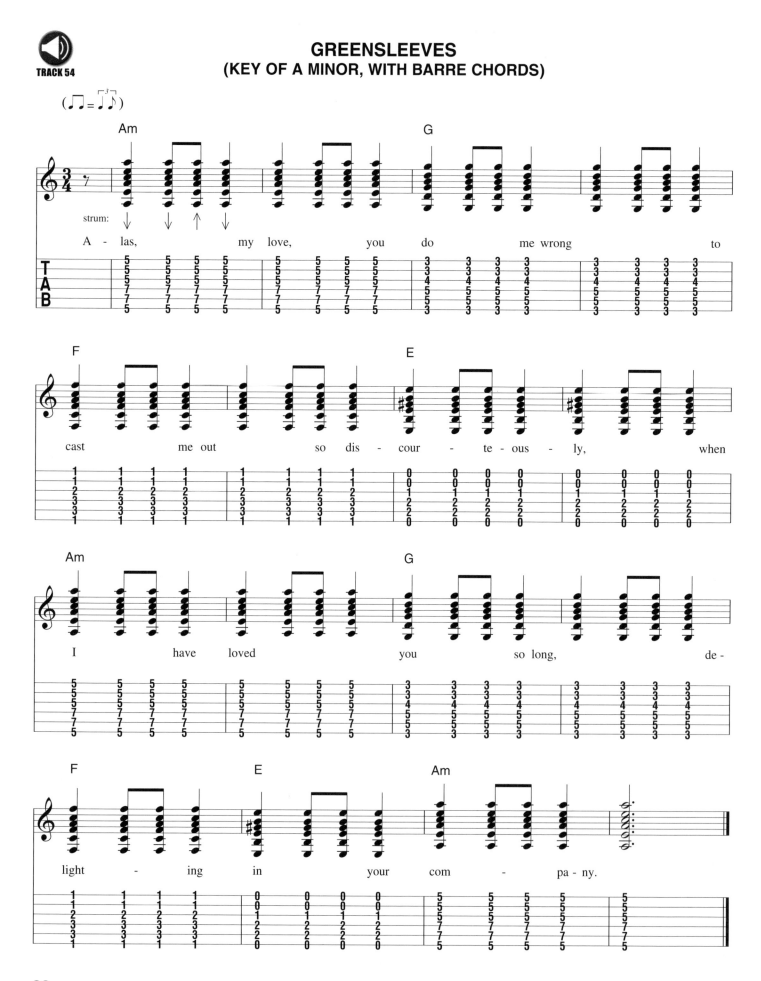

GREENSLEEVES
(KEY OF A MINOR, WITH BARRE CHORDS)

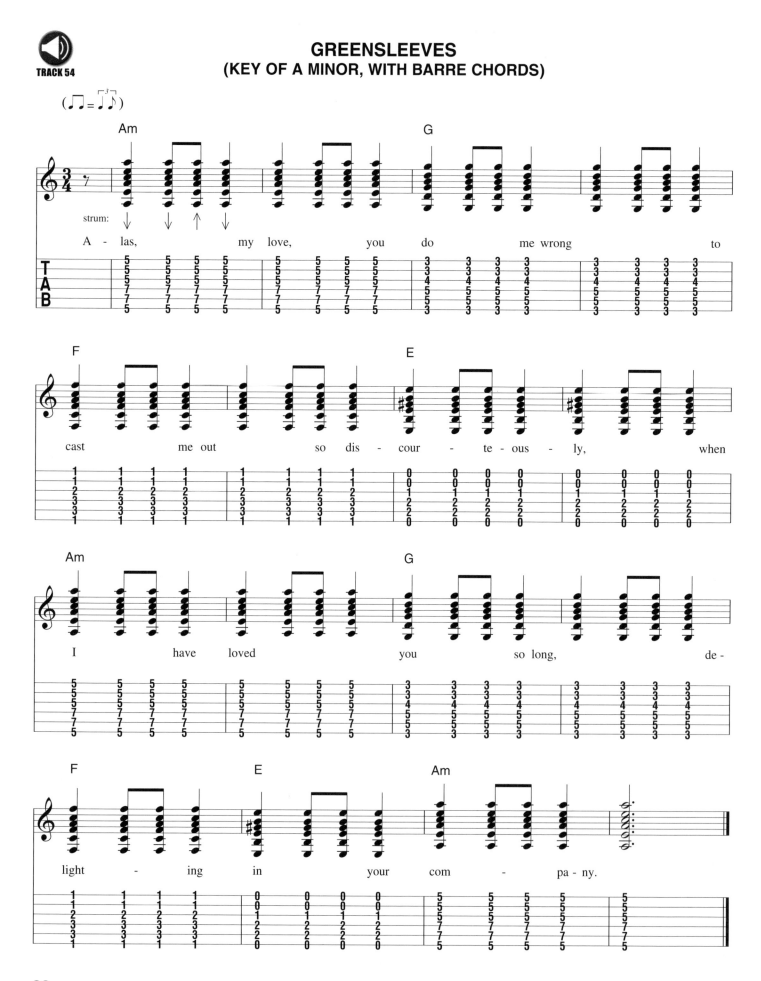

By using major barre chords, you can play in any key. The following arrangement of the American Civil War song "Aura Lee" is in the key of B♭ major and contains five chords, all played as moveable sixth- or fifth-string-root chords. The tune may sound familiar, as it was the basis for Elvis Presley's "Love Me Tender." Remember, the location of each chord can be found by its fifth- or sixth-string root note.

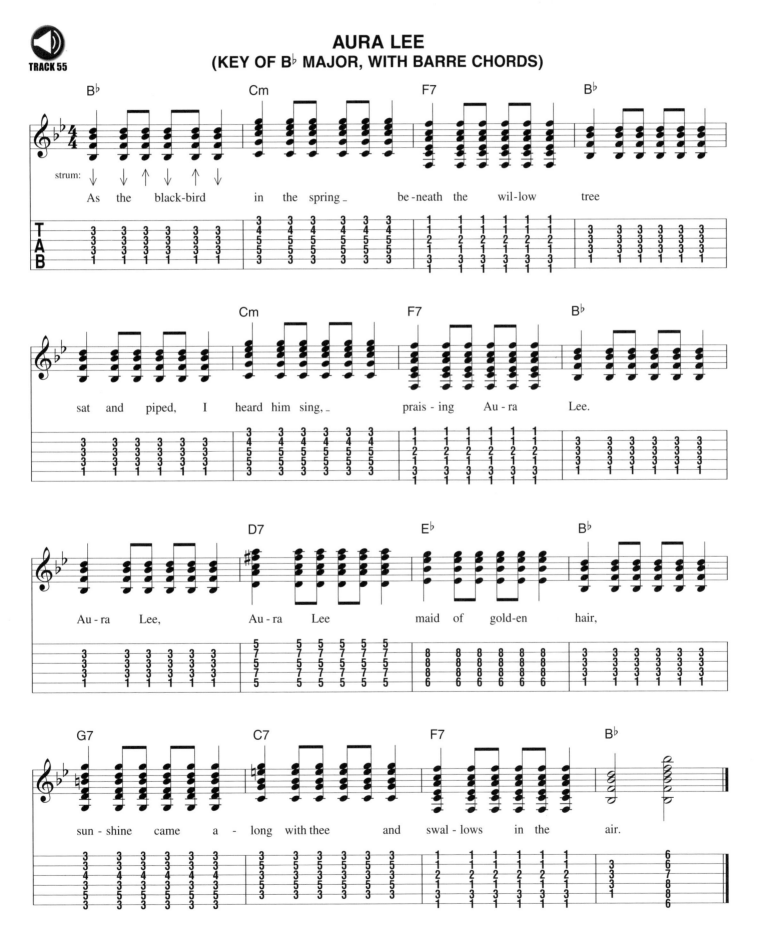

SUMMING UP—NOW YOU KNOW...

1. How to play barred (moveable) major, minor, and seventh chords with a sixth-string root.

2. How to play barred (moveable) major, minor, and seventh chords with a fifth-string root.

3. How to play barre chords all over the fretboard.

4. How to play moveable power chords and boogie licks.

HOW TO READ MUSIC

Many excellent guitarists never learn to read standard music notation. But those who do learn have several advantages: they can sing or play melodies by reading from a book and they can learn songs or solos more quickly. Unlike tablature, music notation includes *timing*, a very important element in music.

THE NOTES

Here are the musical notes of the staff (the five lines and four spaces above the tab staff) and how they relate to tablature:

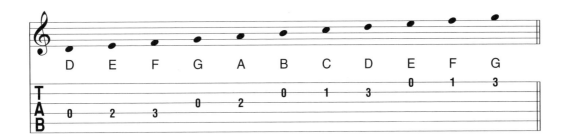

Notes are located below and above the staff, as well:

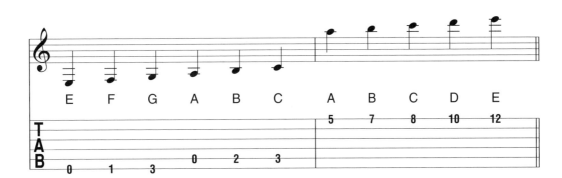

Sharps are indicated by a sharp sign (♯) that precedes the notehead, and flats are indicated by a flat sign (♭):

Although the C major scale contains no sharps or flats, every other key includes at least one sharp or flat. Every piece of music begins with a *key signature*, which tells you which key the music is in and which sharps or flats are in that key. For example, the G major scale has one sharp in its major scale (F♯), so the key signature for G looks like this:

The sharp sign (♯) is located on F (the top line) on the musical staff, so all F notes will be played as F♯ throughout the tune.

Here are the key signatures for the keys used in this book:

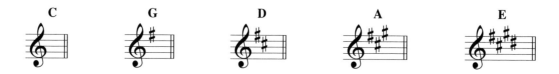

TIMING

The musical staff is divided into *measures* (or "bars") via vertical lines:

Each bar has a predetermined number of beats, indicated by a *time signature*, which is written at the beginning of a piece of music, after the key signature:

"4/4" means: four beats per bar, with quarter notes (see next page) receiving the value of one beat.

"3/4" means: three beats per bar, with quarter notes receiving one beat.

"6/8" means: six beats per bar, with eighth notes (see next page) receiving one beat.

Notes have various time values:

    A quarter note (♩) = one beat of 4/4 time

    An eighth note (♪) = half the length of a quarter note

    Two eighth notes (♫) = one quarter note

    A half note (♩) = twice the length of a quarter note

    A whole note (o) = twice the length of a half note

Here are some sample bars of 4/4 and 3/4 time, with counting prompts provided below the staff:

Rests, which indicate a pause between notes, possess various time values, as well:

    A quarter rest (𝄽) = one beat of 4/4 time

    An eighth rest (𝄾) = half the length of a quarter rest

    A half rest (–) = twice the length of a quarter rest

    A whole rest (▬) = twice the length of a half rest

Here are some sample bars of 4/4 and 3/4 time, with counting prompts provided below the staff:

Some notes are *dotted*, which increases their value by one half:

    ♩. = a quarter note plus an eighth note

    ♩. = a half note plus a quarter note (or three quarter notes)

Here are sample bars of 4/4 and 3/4 time that include dotted notes:

Repeat signs, located at the beginning and at the end of a musical phrase, tell you to repeat that phrase. Any number of bars of music can be enclosed by repeat signs:

Sometimes, a repeated musical phrase has two different endings, as indicated below:

Here's how to read the above five bars: First, play the first four bars (including the first ending); then, play the first three bars again, skipping the first ending in favor of the second ending. To help clarify, the bars are numbered above the staff; the repeat signs and first and second endings direct you to play the measures in the following sequence: 1–2–3–4, 1–2–3–5.

While many other subtle musical notations exist, this quick summary should get you started reading music. The musical example below will help you relate musical notes on the staff to the guitar fretboard:

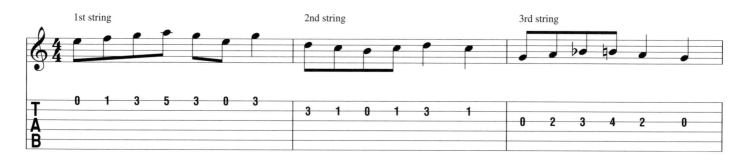

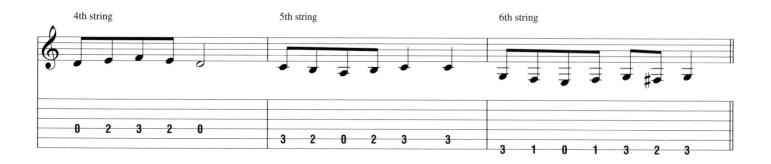

WHAT'S NEXT?

Once you're comfortable with the chords, strums, scales, and picking and strumming patterns in this book, you'll probably want to keep learning to progress to a higher playing level. Thankfully, Hal Leonard publishes plenty of books and DVDs to help you do so, and one of the best is Fred Sokolow's *Fretboard Roadmaps* (Second Edition), which contains many fretboard patterns that will help you play in any key, all over the fretboard, and offers several soloing strategies.

After that, it's helpful to choose a particular genre, such as rock, blues, country, jazz, classical, bluegrass, or rockabilly. To get you started, you may want to work through one of Sokolow's *Roadmaps* books (with CDs) that focuses on your chosen genre(s), such as:

Fretboard Roadmaps for Rock Guitar

Fretboard Roadmaps for Blues Guitar

Fretboard Roadmaps for Country Guitar

Fretboard Roadmaps for Jazz Guitar

Fretboard Roadmaps for Slide Guitar

Fretboard Roadmaps for Bluegrass and Folk Guitar

Fretboard Roadmaps for Acoustic Guitar

Fretboard Roadmaps for Alternate Guitar Tunings

The *Roadmaps* books teach you how to improvise in a particular style (blues, rock, etc.) and how to navigate the guitar neck in that genre.

Other excellent methods by Sokolow include:

Basic Blues for Guitar (book/CD)

Basic Fingerpicking Guitar (book/CD)

Improvising Lead Guitar (book/CD)

Fretboard Roadmaps for Guitar (DVD)

Hal Leonard Bluegrass Guitar Method (book/CD)

Hal Leonard Rockabilly Guitar Method (book/CD)

Hal Leonard Folk Guitar Method (book/CD)

As soon as you can, find other guitar players to jam with. It's especially helpful to jam with someone who plays at a higher level than you—but will put up with your learning curve! It's an excellent and fun way to progress as a player.

Good luck!

Fred Sokolow
Sokolowmusic.com

TRACK SHEET/SONG INDEX

ABOUT THE AUTHOR

FRED SOKOLOW is a versatile "musician's musician." Besides fronting his own jazz, bluegrass, and rock bands, Fred has toured with Bobbie Gentry, Jim Stafford, Tom Paxton, Ian Whitcomb, Jody Stecher, and the Limeliters, playing guitar, banjo, mandolin, and Dobro. His music has been heard on many TV shows (*Survivor*, *Dr. Quinn*), commercials, and movies (listen for his Dixieland-style banjo in *The Cat's Meow*).

Sokolow has written nearly a hundred stringed instrument books and videos for seven major publishers. This library of instructional material, which teaches jazz, rock, bluegrass, country, and blues guitar, banjo, Dobro, and mandolin, is sold on six continents. He also teaches musical seminars on the West Coast. Two jazz CDs, two rock guitar and two banjo recordings, which showcase Sokolow's technique, all received excellent reviews in the U.S. and Europe.

If you think Sokolow still isn't versatile enough, know that he emceed for Carol Doda at San Francisco's legendary Condor Club, accompanied a Russian balalaika virtuoso at the swank Bonaventure Hotel in L.A., won the *Gong Show*, played lap steel and banjo on the *Tonight Show*, picked Dobro with Chubby Checker, and played mandolin with Rick James.

For any questions that you may have about this book or other Fred Sokolow books, please visit www.sokolowmusic.com.